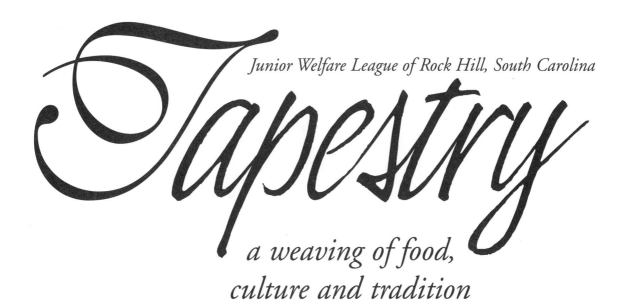

Tapestry

Junior Welfare League of Rock Hill, South Carolina

a weaving of food, culture and tradition

Tapestry

a weaving of food, culture and tradition

Copyright © 2000
The Junior Welfare League of Rock Hill
P. O. Box 3211
Rock Hill, South Carolina 29732

Library of Congress Number: 00-131128
ISBN: 0-9679156-0-0

Designed, Edited, and Manufactured by
Favorite Recipes® Press
an imprint of

FRP

P.O. Box 305142
Nashville, Tennessee 37230
1-800-358-0560

Book Design: Jim Scott
Project Manager: Susan Larson
Art Director: Steve Newman
Managing Editor: Mary Cummings

Manufactured in the United States of America
First Printing: 2000   8000 copies

Contents

Acknowledgements

About the Cover Art:

Genie Wilder *Another Time*

"Most of my life I've strived to be an artist. Growing up in Rock Hill among my family of six, we all shared a love of creativity. Several years ago this led to a series of paintings featuring family photos. "These family photos are of my mother (Harriet Marshall, first president of the Junior Welfare League) and me, her brother, my 'Uncle Buddy,' Mother at the age of twelve, and my father with his childhood nurse.

"These paintings of my family were mingled with fruit, vegetables, flowers, and familiar objects from home. As I become more involved with the act of painting, these inanimate objects seem almost human and stories begin to unfold. To quote Edward Hopper, 'If you could say it in words, there would be no reason to paint.'"

About the Artist

Genie Marshall Wilder, born and raised in Rock Hill, is a member of a large, creative family and has painted for most of her life. She has published numerous limited edition prints of her paintings and has won many awards and honors for her work, including first place from the South Carolina Watercolor Society and an Award of Excellence from the Midwest Watercolor Society. Her work can be seen in private and corporate collections around the world.

Cookbook Committee 1999–2000

Mrs. Edward A. Brock (Kim), Chairperson

Mrs. Michael W. Climer (Kim)

Mrs. Cameron S. Davidson (Amy)

Mrs. Robert J. Holmes, Jr. (Nancy)

Mrs. Steven J. Knight (Lisa)

Mrs. William G. McCarthy, Jr. (Sheila)

Mrs. Richard B. Norwood (Laura)

Mrs. Richard O. Poag (Pam)

Mrs. John C. Pollok (Maura)

Mrs. John E. Reese III (Carrie)

Mrs. Samuel W. Rhodes, Jr. (Julie)

Mrs. James W. Sheedy (Elizabeth)

Research Committee 1997–1999

Mrs. Wilmot C. Burch (Ann)

Mrs. H. Leon Comer, Jr. (Judy)

Mrs. Cameron S. Davidson (Amy)

Mrs. Leland B. Greeley (Sabella)

Mrs. A. Watts Huckabee (Gina)

Mrs. James M. Mahon (Daphne)

Mrs. Richard O. Poag (Pam)

Mrs. Samuel W. Rhodes, Jr. (Julie)

Introduction

SPECIAL THANKS TO SHEILA WEST MCCARTHY FOR WRITING THE SIDEBARS
AND SPECIAL INTEREST INFORMATION INCLUDED IN THIS COOKBOOK.

When discussing the title for the Junior Welfare League of Rock Hill's first cookbook, our committee was faced with a dilemma: How can we honor the contributions of Rock Hillians that have come before us and reflect the ever-changing makeup of this "New South" community?

Rock Hill, just twenty miles south of Charlotte, North Carolina, is located in York County, one of South Carolina's fastest growing communities. Before this burst of economic and population expansion, Rock Hill was a small southern town with a rich textile heritage. Woven into our social fabric are hardworking, churchgoing people who value the sanctity of home and family. Somehow, Rock Hillians have been able to manage and accept inevitable growth but maintain their sense of balance.

This sense of knowing and maintaining what is important may be what draws so many people to move here and to neighboring areas. Weary of the mindless hustle and bustle which is now so much a part of everyday life, new residents from all over the country have found a "HOME" in Rock Hill. Many have brought new ideas and have made positive contributions to the community. But still, the common threads that unite us are one and the same: family, faith, and home.

The tapestry of our community is evident through the recipes and design of this cookbook. There are gourmet cooks, southern cooks, family cooks, and those who just want to get a hot meal on the table. Some of these cooks entertain in their homes while others entertain in a business setting. You will find a delightful assortment of recipes that reflect the lifestyles of our contributors.

The artwork on the *Tapestry* cover and chapter openers was chosen to display Rock Hill's vibrant art community. Local artists and Cookbook Committee members worked to choose artwork that would be significant to the cookbook and help to illustrate Rock Hill's *Tapestry*. Possibly, the talents of these artists will inspire cooks to treat each recipe as an artistic creation!

Sheila West McCarthy

Corporate Sponsors

We gratefully acknowledge the financial assistance of the following corporations and their concern for children and families in our community.

SPENCER & SPENCER, P.A. ATTORNEYS AND COUNSELORS AT LAW

Sponsors

PATRONS

Mr. & Mrs. Charles J. Bowers
Mr. & Mrs. Gary T. Brannan
Mr. & Mrs. Edward A. Brock
Designs of Jeannine Burger, Inc.
Dr. & Mrs. Dennis M. Clemens
Mr. & Mrs. Michael W. Climer
Mr. & Mrs. H. Leon Comer, Jr.
Mr. & Mrs. Coy F. Coulson
Dr. & Mrs. William L. Culp, Jr.
Mr. & Mrs. Cameron S. Davidson
Dr. & Mrs. Anthony J. DiGiorgio
Mr. & Mrs. Malcolm D. Faulkenberry
Mr. & Mrs. Craig T. Ferguson
Fort Mill Pharmacy
Dr. & Mrs. Robert V. Fulmer
Mr. & Mrs. Tom S. Gettys

Mr. & Mrs. Charles W. Hall
Dr. & Mrs. Harry E. Hicklin III
Mr. & Mrs. C. Marion Hicklin
Mr. & Mrs. John S. Holladay
Mr. & Mrs. Robert J. Holmes, Jr.
Rev. & Mrs. Thomas F. Hudson
Dr. & Mrs. Mark L. Landrum
Legacy's Child & By Design
Mr. & Mrs. Jimmie C. Matthews
Dr. & Mrs. William G. McCarthy, Jr.
Mr. & Mrs. Thomas A. McKinney
Mr. & Mrs. Kyle E. Melton
Mr. & Mrs. F. Thomas Merritt, Jr.
Mr. & Mrs. Carlisle C. Moore, Jr.
Mr. & Mrs. Carlisle C. Moore III
Dr. & Mrs. Alan M. Nichols

Mr. & Mrs. Richard O. Poag
Dr. & Mrs. E. Neal Powell, Jr.
Dr. & Mrs. John E. Reese III
Mr. & Mrs. Samuel W. Rhodes, Jr.
Mr. & Mrs. John D. Rinehart, Jr.
Mr. & Mrs. Irwin Speizer
Mr. & Mrs. E. Ned Stafford, Jr.
Ms. Anne S. Suite
Mr. & Mrs. Harold P. Tuttle, Jr.
Mr. & Mrs. Roy E. Watkins III
Mr. & Mrs. Frank M. Wilkerson, Jr.
Mr. & Mrs. C. Richard Williams
Mrs. Kathleen Patrick Wilson
Mr. & Mrs. D. Douglas Woods

CONTRIBUTORS

Mrs. C.H. Albright
Mr. & Mrs. Bryant G. Barnes
Mr. & Mrs. John M. Barnes, Jr.
Dr. & Mrs. Jeff Blank
Mr. & Mrs. Joseph M. Brice
Mr. & Mrs. R. V. Bridges, Jr.
Burnette & Payne, P.A.
Mr. & Mrs. Donald W. Carter
Mr. & Mrs. David D. Casey
Mr. & Mrs. Charles B. Cauthen
Mr. & Mrs. Rea K. Cauthen
Mr. & Mrs. Harry A. Dest
Dr. & Mrs. Hugh B. Dickey III
Mr. & Mrs. Jefferson R. Dill

Mr. & Mrs. Terry L. Dodge
Mr. & Mrs. Larry C. Doggett
Mr. & Mrs. Fredrick M. Faircloth, Jr.
Dr. & Mrs. Frank P. Gaston
Mrs. Maggie G. Haddad
Mr. & Mrs. James C. Hardin
Mr. & Mrs. Dana L. Harkness
Mrs. Mary Ann Hoffman
Ms. Virginia J. Kellett
Mr. & Mrs. Albert G. LeRoy
Mr. & Mrs. David C. Leslie, Jr.
Mr. & Mrs. P. David Lloyd, Jr.
Mr. & Mrs. R. H. MacKintosh
Mr. & Mrs. Thomas E. Martin

Ms. Katherine Morgan
Mr. & Mrs. Houston O. Motz, Jr.
Mr. & Mrs. J. D. Pilcher, Jr.
Mrs. William W. Rader
Mr. & Mrs. James C. Rhea III
Mr. & Mrs. David M. Rodgers
Dr. & Mrs. Christopher W. Schroeder
Dr. & Mrs. Robert Scoville
Dr. & Mrs. James L. Simpson
Mr. & Mrs. Kenneth B. Smith
Mr. & Mrs. Drenner M. Tinsley
Dr. & Mrs. R. Glen Willis
Mr. & Mrs. C. Y. Workman, Jr.
Mrs. N. Felix Yorke

Prayer and Mission

PRAYER OF SERVICE

We pray that we may never be so tired
That our small world is all we ever see;
Or so supremely satisfied
That what we are is all we want to be.

Give us the joy of filling someone's need;
Make us gracious followers;
make gracious those who lead.
But more than all,
we pray that through the years
We will remember that there
are always new frontiers.

Reprinted from the Handbook of the National Junior League

MISSION STATEMENT

The Junior Welfare League of Rock Hill, Inc. is an organization
of trained volunteers committed to serving and improving the quality of life
for people living in York County.

We are dedicated to focusing on advocacy, health,
education and awareness of issues for children. Our purpose is
exclusively educational and charitable.

Established in 1998

Rhapsody in Blue
Peggy Rivers

Appetizers & Beverages

Peggy Rivers

Peggy Rivers' Rhapsody in Blue *is painted in oil. From her Martini series, this work was painted for one of her dear friends.*

Peggy Rivers, a Rock Hill resident, did her first oil painting at the age of twelve. A wife, mother, and working artist, she now manages a local art gallery and is a university art instructor.

Peggy's work has won numerous awards and honors, and has been exhibited throughout the United States.

Ham Delights

1 pound cooked ham	1 cup packed brown sugar
1½ pounds bulk sausage	1 teaspoon dry mustard
2 cups cracker crumbs	½ cup white vinegar
2 eggs, beaten	½ cup hot water
1 cup milk	¼ cup raisins

- Cut the ham into pieces. Place in a food processor container fitted with a steel blade. Process until finely ground. Combine with the sausage, cracker crumbs, eggs and milk in a bowl and mix well. Shape into 1-inch balls. Place in a shallow baking dish.
- Bake at 350 degrees for 10 minutes. Combine the brown sugar, dry mustard, vinegar, water and raisins in a bowl. Stir until the sugar is dissolved. Pour over the ham balls. Bake for 40 minutes, basting often. You may freeze these and reheat.
- *Yield: 10 servings*

Bacon and Cheese Snacks

2 cups grated cheese	2 tablespoons finely chopped
1 (2-ounce) jar	onion
bacon bits	1 (40-slice) package party
1 cup mayonnaise	rye bread

- Combine the cheese, bacon bits, mayonnaise and onion in a bowl and mix well. Spread over one side of each slice of bread. Place the bread, spread side up, on a baking sheet. Bake at 325 degrees for 15 minutes.
- *Yield: 12 to 14 servings*

MORNING DROP IN

For a great way to honor a new neighbor or just catch up on the latest with your friends, prepare a Morning Drop In. Create a coffee bar by having insulated carafes of flavored gourmet coffees from which to choose. The food is fairly simple and can be placed on the table shortly before the party. This frees the hostess to enjoy her guests.

Ham Delights

Bacon and Cheese Snacks

Danish Pastries

Cheese Cookies

Sour Cream Pound Cake

Roquefort Grapes

Turkey and Chutney Rolls

4 (20-count) packages party rolls in foil trays
8 ounces cream cheese, softened
2 tablespoons mayonnaise
2 tablespoons sour cream
2 tablespoons (heaping) chutney
1 tablespoon Dijon mustard
1/2 to 1 teaspoon curry powder
1/2 to 3/4 teaspoon red pepper
2 to 3 tablespoons minced onion
1/2 (16-ounce) can whole cranberry sauce
1 pound smoked turkey, thinly sliced

- Remove the rolls from the trays. Slice each package of rolls in half horizontally; do not individually separate.
- Combine the cream cheese, mayonnaise, sour cream, chutney, mustard, curry powder and red pepper in a medium bowl and mix well. Combine the onion and cranberry sauce in a bowl and mix well. Spread a thin layer of the cream cheese mixture over the top and bottom of each package of rolls.
- Layer one-fourth of the turkey slices over the bottom of each package of rolls. Spread a thin layer of the cranberry mixture over the turkey layers. Place the top halves of the rolls over the bottom halves. Cut the rolls into individual sandwiches and place back into the aluminum trays.
- Bake, covered, at 350 degrees for 20 to 25 minutes or until warm, removing the cover for the last 10 minutes if desired. You may freeze these and reheat.
- *Yield: 80 sandwiches*

Crab Cakes

Mrs. John M. Barnes (Jean), Past President, 1961–1962

2 eggs
1 tablespoon Dijon mustard
1 tablespoon lemon juice
1 tablespoon Worcestershire sauce
1 tablespoon mayonnaise
1 tablespoon margarine or butter, melted
1 tablespoon chopped parsley
1 to 2 teaspoons prepared horseradish
1 cup bread crumbs
1 pound claw crab meat
Salt to taste
1/4 cup vegetable oil

- Combine the eggs, mustard, lemon juice, Worcestershire sauce, mayonnaise, margarine, parsley, horseradish and a small amount of the bread crumbs in a bowl and mix well.
- Add the crab meat and mix well. Season with the salt. Shape into 8 large cakes. Dredge in the remaining bread crumbs. Heat the oil in a skillet. Cook the crab cakes in the hot oil until brown on both sides and cooked through.
- *Yield: 4 servings*

The Museum of York County hosted two Sotheby's Discovery Days (a fore-runner of the PBS series Antiques Roadshow). We served the appraisers these crab cakes and a good dose of southern hospitality. We also served them pimento cheese sandwiches which they had not had before: it's a southern thing.

—Mrs. W. C. Spencer (Ann Audrey)

Lamplighter Crab Cakes

Mrs. W. C. Spencer (Ann Audrey), Past President, 1974–1975

1 egg white	**¼ cup bread crumbs**
1 cup mayonnaise	**1 pound back fin crab meat**
⅛ teaspoon seafood seasoning	**¾ cup bread crumbs**
⅛ teaspoon cayenne pepper	**Vegetable oil for frying**
1 teaspoon lemon juice	

- Combine the egg white, mayonnaise, seafood seasoning, cayenne pepper, lemon juice and ¼ cup bread crumbs in a bowl and mix well. Add the crab meat and mix well. Shape into 12 cakes. Dredge in the ¾ cup bread crumbs. Heat the oil in a skillet. Cook the crab cakes in the hot oil until brown on both sides and cooked through.
- *Yield: 6 servings*

Crabbies

Mrs. W. A. Barron (Bess Dargon), Past President, 1952–1953

½ cup (1 stick) butter, softened	**8 ounces crab meat**
1 (5-ounce) jar Old English cheese spread	**Dash of Tabasco sauce**
1½ teaspoons mayonnaise	**6 English muffins, split**
½ teaspoon garlic salt	**Paprika to taste**

- Combine the butter, cheese spread, mayonnaise, garlic salt, crab meat and Tabasco sauce in a bowl and mix well. Spread over the muffin halves. Freeze, covered, until frozen through. Cut each muffin half into 6 or 8 wedges. Sprinkle the paprika over the tops. Place on a baking sheet. Bake at 350 degrees until bubbly.
- *Yield: 72 to 96 appetizers*

Shrimp Deviled Eggs

4 ounces frozen cooked salad
   shrimp, thawed
4 hard-cooked eggs

$1/4$ to $1/2$ cup mayonnaise
Salt and pepper to taste
Paprika to taste

- Set aside 8 of the best looking shrimp. Chop the remaining shrimp coarsely. Place on paper towels and press to remove the excess moisture. Cut the eggs in half lengthwise. Remove the egg yolks and place in a bowl, being careful not to break the egg whites. Mash the egg yolks. Add the chopped shrimp, mayonnaise, salt and pepper and mix well. Spoon into the egg white halves. Sprinkle with the paprika. Place one of the reserved shrimp on top of each deviled egg.
- *Yield: 8 appetizers*

Special Shrimp Sea Island

5 pounds shrimp, peeled,
   deveined, cooked
10 mild white onions,
   cut into rings
2 cups olive oil
$1^{1}/2$ cups cider vinegar

1 (3-ounce) jar capers
Salt to taste
Sugar to taste
Tabasco sauce to taste
Worcestershire sauce to taste

- Alternate layers of shrimp and onions in a deep flat pan until all ingredients are used. Combine the olive oil, vinegar, capers, salt, sugar, Tabasco sauce and Worcestershire sauce in a bowl and mix well. Pour over the layers. Marinate, tightly covered, in the refrigerator for 12 hours or longer; drain. Arrange on a serving platter. Serve with wooden picks.
- *Yield: 20 servings*

PAST PRESIDENTS

Past President Bess Barron got the recipe Crabbies from Kathleen Stans, wife of Maurice Stans. The Stans Foundation was the principal private benefactor of the Museum of York County for many years and the donor of the Stans African Collection. At a reception in their honor, Mrs. Stans gave the MYCO staff a tip. Always wear your nametag on the right side. It is easier to steal a glimpse of the tag when it is worn on the right side.

—Mrs. W. A. Barron (Bess Dargon)

Sixteen women met for an organizational meeting of the Rock Hill Charity League on August 10, 1938, at the home of future president, Mrs. Arnold Marshall (Harriet). The next week they met and collected thirty-six dollars in dues, formed a welfare committee to investigate service needs of agencies and organizations, proposed additional members, and determined that thirty-six hours of service each month would be a membership requirement.

Artichoke Nibbles

2 (6-ounce) jars marinated artichokes
1 small onion, chopped
1 garlic clove, minced
4 eggs, beaten
¼ cup fine bread crumbs
¼ teaspoon salt
⅛ teaspoon pepper
⅛ teaspoon oregano
⅛ teaspoon Tabasco sauce
8 ounces sharp Cheddar cheese, shredded
2 tablespoons minced parsley

- Drain 1 jar of the artichokes, reserving the marinade. Drain the remaining jar of artichokes, discarding the marinade. Chop the artichokes and set aside.
- Sauté the onion and garlic in the reserved marinade in a skillet for 5 minutes. Combine with the eggs, bread crumbs, salt, pepper, oregano, Tabasco sauce, cheese, parsley and artichokes in a large bowl and mix well. Spoon into a greased 7×11-inch baking pan.
- Bake at 350 degrees for 30 minutes or until set. Cool in the pan. Cut into 1-inch squares. You may serve these cold or reheat at 325 degrees for 10 to 12 minutes.
- *Yield: 4 dozen*

Roquefort Grapes

1½ cups walnuts
8 ounces cream cheese,
  softened

2 to 3 ounces Roquefort or
  bleu cheese
1 pound seedless grapes

- Spread the walnuts on a baking sheet. Bake at 300 degrees for 5 to
  7 minutes or until toasted. Remove from baking sheet and chop.
- Combine the cream cheese and Roquefort cheese in a mixing bowl and
  beat until smooth. Add the grapes and stir gently until well coated. Place
  the grapes on a baking sheet. Chill for 30 minutes.
- Roll the grapes in the toasted walnuts to coat. Arrange on a tray to
  resemble a cluster of grapes. Garnish with grape leaves.
- *Yield: 4 to 6 servings*

Marinated Mushrooms

1 pound small whole
  mushrooms
¼ cup light olive oil
¼ cup lemon or lime juice
2 green onions, finely chopped

1 garlic clove, pressed
⅛ teaspoon white pepper
¼ teaspoon salt
¼ teaspoon parsley
Paprika to taste

- Arrange the mushrooms in a flat shallow dish. Combine the olive
  oil, lemon juice, green onions, garlic, white pepper, salt, parsley and
  paprika in a bowl and mix well. Pour over the mushrooms. Marinate,
  covered, in the refrigerator for 14 to 16 hours. Stir before serving.
  Serve with wooden picks.
- *Yield: 6 to 8 servings*

Walnut-Stuffed Mushrooms

18 large mushrooms
2 tablespoons butter, melted
Garlic salt to taste
2 tablespoons minced onion
1 tablespoon mayonnaise

2 tablespoons Worcestershire
  sauce
3 tablespoons grated Parmesan
  cheese
¹/₄ cup finely chopped walnuts

- Remove the stems from the mushrooms and reserve. Brush the caps with a small amount of the melted butter. Sprinkle with garlic salt.
- Chop the reserved mushroom stems. Sauté in the remaining butter with the onion in a skillet. Combine the mushroom mixture, mayonnaise, Worcestershire sauce, cheese and walnuts in a bowl and mix well. Fill the mushroom caps with the mixture.
- Arrange the filled caps on a baking sheet. Bake at 400 degrees for 10 minutes or until mushrooms are tender and tops are brown. You may double or triple this to use as a main dish.
- *Yield: 9 servings*

Cheese Cookies

1 cup (2 sticks) butter, softened
10 ounces sharp Cheddar cheese,
  shredded, softened
2 cups self-rising flour
1 teaspoon salt

1 teaspoon paprika
¹/₂ teaspoon dry mustard
1 teaspoon garlic chile sauce
  (optional)
1¹/₂ cups chopped pecans

- Cream the butter and cheese in a mixing bowl. Add the flour gradually, mixing well after each addition. Add the salt, paprika, dry mustard and chile sauce and mix well. Fold in the pecans. Shape the cheese mixture into 1-inch balls. Place on a cookie sheet. Flatten with a fork making a crisscross pattern. Bake at 400 degrees for 15 minutes.
- *Yield: 3 dozen*

Cream Cheese Swirls

8 ounces cream cheese, softened
2 tablespoons finely chopped onion
1 teaspoon milk
5 slices bacon, crisp-cooked, crumbled, or 3 tablespoons bacon bits
2 (8-count) packages refrigerated crescent rolls
Grated Parmesan cheese

- Combine the cream cheese, onion and milk in a bowl and mix well. Stir in the bacon.
- Unroll the crescent rolls into 8 rectangles, pressing the perforations to seal. Spread the cream cheese mixture over each rectangle. Roll to enclose the filling, starting at the long side. Seal the ends. Cut each roll into 8 pieces.
- Arrange, cut-side down, on a baking sheet. Sprinkle with the Parmesan cheese. Bake at 375 degrees for 10 to 12 minutes or until golden brown. You may use light cream cheese.
- *Yield: 64 appetizers*

Cheese Straws

1 pound sharp Cheddar cheese,
   shredded
2¼ cups cake flour
1⅔ sticks butter, melted

7 to 10 dashes Tabasco sauce, or
   to taste
Salt to taste

- Combine the cheese, flour, butter and Tabasco sauce in a bowl and mix well. Knead until smooth; do not add additional flour.
- Shape into a log. Chill, tightly wrapped, in the refrigerator. Cut into ¼-inch slices. Place on a baking sheet. You may place the dough in a cookie press fitted with a star tip and press onto a baking sheet. Sprinkle with salt. Bake at 250 degrees for 40 minutes or until brown.
- *Yield: 2½ dozen*

Apple Cheese Ball

8 ounces white Cheddar cheese,
   shredded
8 ounces cream cheese, softened
1 teaspoon garlic powder

⅛ teaspoon ground red pepper
Paprika
1 (1½-inch) cinnamon stick
1 bay leaf

- Process the Cheddar cheese, cream cheese, garlic powder and red pepper in a food processor until smooth, scraping down the sides. Chill, covered, for 30 minutes. Shape into a ball, making an indentation in the top to resemble an apple. Chill, covered, for 30 minutes. Coat heavily with the paprika. Chill, covered, for 1 hour.
- Insert the cinnamon stick and bay leaf into the indentation to resemble an apple stem and leaf. Serve with assorted crackers.
- *Yield: 2 cups*

Brattonsville Cheese Mold

1 pound sharp Cheddar cheese, shredded
1 cup chopped pecans
1 small onion, grated
³/₄ cup mayonnaise
¹/₂ teaspoon (or more) minced garlic
¹/₂ teaspoon (or more) Tabasco sauce
Strawberry preserves

- Line a round mold with plastic wrap. Combine the cheese, pecans, onion, mayonnaise, garlic and Tabasco sauce in a bowl and mix well. Spoon into the prepared mold. Chill, covered, in the refrigerator.
- Unmold onto a serving plate. Spoon the strawberry preserves over the top. Serve with crackers.
- *Yield: 16 servings*

Cool Summer Cheese Ball

2 cups chopped pecans
16 ounces cream cheese, softened
1 (8-ounce) can crushed pineapple, drained
¹/₄ cup chopped green bell pepper
2 tablespoons chopped onion
1 tablespoon seasoned salt

- Set aside a small amount of the pecans. Combine the remaining pecans, cream cheese, pineapple, bell pepper, onion and seasoned salt in a bowl and mix well.
- Shape into a ball. Roll in the reserved pecans to coat. Chill, covered, for 3 hours or longer. Serve with crackers or toasted bagels.
- *Yield: 8 to 12 servings*

THE WAR EFFORT

During World War II, the Junior Welfare League of Rock Hill suddenly had a list of nonresident members as wives went off to live on army bases with their husbands. League members at home joined the war effort in 1941. They operated the lunchroom and served meals at the old armory for soldiers on maneuvers in South Carolina. Also, they worked in the concession stand, served as USO hostesses and gave money for National Defense organizations. They volunteered for the Red Cross, packed Christmas kits for soldiers, made surgical dressings, and raised money for the War Fund. Scrapbooks were made for soldiers. After World War II, the League sent packages to veterans in hospitals. In 1967 the League again joined the war effort by bringing articles for "ditty bags" for Vietnam soldiers.

VERNON GRANT

Nationally known artist and illustrator Vernon Grant, creator of the famous Kellogg's gnomes "Snap! Crackle! Pop!©," moved to Rock Hill in the 1940s with his wife, Lib Fewell. You can see exhibits of his work, including his Santas, at Christmastime at the Museum of York County. Together with C. H. "Ickey" Albright, he established Rock Hill's "Come See Me" festival and created its mascot, Glen the Frog.

Feta Cheese Ball

8 ounces cream cheese, softened
4 to 6 ounces feta cheese
1 tablespoon sour cream
1 teaspoon dillweed
1/2 teaspoon oregano
1/4 teaspoon pepper
1 small garlic clove, pressed or minced
2 medium green onions, tops only, minced
Salt to taste
5 large radishes, shredded
2 tablespoons minced parsley

- Line a 1 1/2-cup bowl with plastic wrap. Combine the cream cheese, feta cheese, sour cream, dillweed, oregano and pepper in a bowl and mix until smooth and creamy. Stir in the garlic and green onions. Season with the salt. Spoon into the prepared bowl. Chill, covered, in the refrigerator.
- Shape into a ball. Remove the plastic wrap. Roll in the radishes to coat. Place on a serving plate. Sprinkle with the parsley. Serve with crackers or toasted pita slices.
- *Yield: 10 to 12 servings*

Parmesan-Coated Brie

1 egg, lightly beaten
1 tablespoon water
1/2 cup Italian bread crumbs
1/4 cup grated Parmesan cheese

1 (15-ounce) wheel of Brie
  with herbs
1/4 cup vegetable oil
Rosemary sprigs for garnish

- Combine the egg and water in a shallow dish and mix well. Combine the bread crumbs and Parmesan cheese in a separate shallow dish and mix well. Dip the Brie in the egg mixture, turning to coat all sides. Roll in the bread crumb mixture to coat. Repeat the process.
- Chill for 1 hour or longer. Heat the oil in a heavy skillet over medium heat. Add the coated Brie. Cook for 2 minutes on each side or until golden brown. Place on a serving plate. Garnish with rosemary sprigs. Serve with sliced bread or crackers.
- *Yield: 6 to 8 servings*

Pinecone Cheese Ball

8 ounces cream cheese, softened
1/2 cup mayonnaise
5 slices bacon, crisp-cooked,
  crumbled
1/8 teaspoon pepper

1 tablespoon chopped
  green onions
1/2 teaspoon (or more) dillweed
1 1/4 cups whole almonds
Pine sprig for garnish

- Combine the cream cheese and mayonnaise in a bowl and mix well. Add the bacon, pepper, green onions and dillweed and mix well. Shape into a pinecone. Wrap in plastic wrap sprayed with nonstick cooking spray. Chill, covered, for 8 to 12 hours.
- Unwrap the pinecone and cover with the almonds, starting at the pointed end. Place a pine sprig in the other end. Serve with crackers.
- *Yield: 8 to 10 servings*

Garlic Feta Cheese Spread

4 ounces feta cheese, crumbled
4 ounces cream cheese, softened
⅓ cup mayonnaise
1 garlic clove, minced

¼ teaspoon basil
¼ teaspoon oregano
⅛ teaspoon dillweed
⅛ teaspoon thyme

- Combine the feta cheese, cream cheese, mayonnaise, garlic, basil, oregano, dillweed and thyme in a bowl and mix well. Spoon into a serving bowl. Serve with crackers.
- *Yield: 32 servings*

Goat Cheese with Sun-Dried Tomatoes and Rosemary

12 sun-dried tomato halves
6 garlic cloves, pressed
¼ cup olive oil
2 tablespoons chopped fresh rosemary, or 2 teaspoons dried rosemary

1 French baguette
Olive oil for brushing
1 (10-ounce) package goat cheese

- Combine the tomatoes with enough boiling water to cover in a bowl. Let stand for 5 minutes. Drain and chop. Combine the tomatoes, garlic, ¼ cup olive oil and rosemary in a bowl and mix well. Chill, covered, for up to 4 hours.
- Cut the baguette into thin slices. Brush each slice with olive oil. Place on a baking sheet. Bake at 350 degrees for 5 minutes or until lightly toasted.
- Place the goat cheese on a serving plate. Spoon the tomato mixture over the goat cheese. Serve with the toasted baguette rounds.
- *Yield: 8 to 10 servings*

Havarti Cheese Spread

20 ounces Havarti cheese,
  shredded, softened
1/4 cup mayonnaise
1/2 cup chopped spring onions

1 (12-ounce) jar seedless
  raspberry jam
1 (5-ounce) package sliced
  almonds

- Combine the cheese and mayonnaise in a bowl and mix until smooth. Stir in the onions. Spoon into a quiche dish. Spread the jam over the cheese mixture.
- Spread the almonds over a baking sheet. Bake at 350 degrees for 15 to 20 minutes or until toasted. Sprinkle over the jam. Serve with crackers.
- *Yield: 12 to 18 servings*

Shrimp Paste Finger Sandwich Spread

8 ounces cream cheese, softened
1 tablespoon lemon juice
1 tablespoon mayonnaise
1/4 teaspoon onion powder
Dash of hot sauce

Pinch of mace
Dash of garlic salt
1 cup finely chopped cooked
  shrimp (about 8 ounces)

- Combine the cream cheese, lemon juice, mayonnaise, onion powder, hot sauce, mace and garlic salt in a bowl and mix well. Stir in the shrimp.
- You may use this as a sandwich filling or shape it into small balls that may then be rolled in chopped parsley or toasted benne seeds.
- *Yield: Spread for 16 to 18 small sandwiches*

*Pimento Cheese Sandwich
Spread makes great
sandwiches for a tailgate
party, soup dinner, or can be
used as an hors d'oeuvre with
Triscuits or Wheat Thins.
This spread also makes a
great ribbon sandwich with
chicken or tuna salad by
alternating wheat and
white bread.*

—Mrs. E. Ned Stafford, Jr.
(Gail Wessinger)

Pimento Cheese Sandwich Spread

Mrs. E. Ned Stafford, Jr. (Gail Wessinger), Past President, 1985–1986

4 to 6 ounces pimentos
1 (2-pound) package Velveeta cheese, shredded
8 ounces cream cheese, softened
3 to 4 tablespoons red wine vinegar
3 to 4 tablespoons sugar
Cayenne pepper to taste
Black pepper to taste
1/2 to 3/4 cup mayonnaise
2 tablespoons (about) cottage cheese or sour cream

- Drain the pimentos, pressing to remove the excess moisture. Beat the pimentos, Velveeta cheese, cream cheese, vinegar, sugar, cayenne pepper and black pepper in a mixing bowl until blended. Add the mayonnaise and mix well. Add enough cottage cheese to make of a smooth and rich consistency. Chill, covered, for 8 to 12 hours.
- You may use this as a sandwich filling, as a spread for crackers or as a layer in a ribbon sandwich.
- *Yield: Spread for 32 sandwiches*

Vegetable Sandwich Spread

1 cucumber
1 green bell pepper
1 tomato
1 carrot

1 small onion
1 envelope unflavored gelatin
2 tablespoons cold water
2 cups mayonnaise

- Chop the cucumber, bell pepper, tomato, carrot and onion finely. Soften the gelatin in the cold water in a large bowl. Add the chopped cucumber, bell pepper, tomato, carrot, onion and mayonnaise and mix well. Chill, covered, in the refrigerator.
- *Yield: Spread for 24 sandwiches*

Artichoke Parmesan Dip

1 cup mayonnaise
1/2 cup sour cream
2 artichoke hearts, chopped
3 teaspoons chopped scallions
1 garlic bulb, minced

1/8 teaspoon salt
1/8 teaspoon pepper
3/4 cup grated Parmesan cheese
1/4 teaspoon Tabasco sauce
1/4 teaspoon lemon juice

- Combine the mayonnaise, sour cream, artichoke hearts, scallions, garlic, salt, pepper, Parmesan cheese, Tabasco sauce and lemon juice in a bowl and mix well. Chill, covered, for 30 to 60 minutes.
- Spoon into a serving bowl. Serve with crackers.
- *Yield: 8 to 10 servings*

APPETIZERS

TEA SANDWICHES

When cutting bread for tea sandwiches, try using an electric knife. You will save time and the bread will have a nice, clean edge. Also, choose a finely textured sandwich bread.

The topping combinations are limitless, but always use only the freshest ingredients. Here are some variations:

Sliced tomato and mashed avocado

Smoked salmon, cream cheese, olive slices and watercress

Smoked turkey and cranberry jelly

Bacon and mashed avocado

Avocado Orange Salsa

2 oranges, coarsely chopped
3 avocados, coarsely chopped
Juice of 3 limes

¹/₂ cup chopped fresh cilantro
1 bunch green onions, chopped
Salt to taste

• Combine the oranges, avocados, lime juice, cilantro and green onions in a bowl and mix well. Season with salt.
• Spoon into a serving bowl. Serve with tortilla chips.
• *Yield: 8 to 10 servings*

Corn Dip

3 ounces Neufchâtel cheese
2 tablespoons sour cream
1 tablespoon mayonnaise
1 tablespoon lime juice
1 cup fresh corn, cooked, mashed

1 bunch spring onions, chopped
1 tablespoon chopped red bell pepper
1 tablespoon chopped fresh cilantro

• Combine the Neufchâtel cheese, sour cream, mayonnaise and lime juice in a bowl and mix until smooth. Add the corn, spring onions, bell pepper and cilantro and mix well.
• Spoon into a serving bowl. Serve with chips.
• *Yield: 6 to 8 servings*

Cucumber Avocado Dip

1 tomato
2 cucumbers
1 avocado

2 cups sour cream
1 envelope Italian salad
  dressing mix

- Peel, seed and chop the tomato. Peel the cucumbers and cut lengthwise. Seed and chop the cucumbers. Drain the tomato and cucumbers. Peel and chop the avocado.
- Combine the sour cream and salad dressing mix in a bowl and mix until smooth. Add the tomato, cucumbers and avocado and mix well. Chill, covered, in the refrigerator. Serve with chips or vegetables.
- *Yield: 10 to 12 servings*

Curry Dip for Fresh Vegetables

^{1}/2 cup mayonnaise
^{1}/2 cup sour cream or yogurt
1 teaspoon curry powder
^{1}/2 teaspoon turmeric
^{1}/4 teaspoon chili powder

^{1}/4 teaspoon ground ginger
^{1}/4 teaspoon paprika
Salt to taste
Cayenne pepper to taste

- Combine the mayonnaise, sour cream, curry powder, turmeric, chili powder, ginger and paprika in a bowl and mix well. Season with salt and cayenne pepper. Chill, covered, for 1 hour or longer. Spoon into a serving bowl.
- *Yield: 6 to 8 servings*

MUSEUMS

The birth of the Museum of York County began when interest grew in establishing a museum in 1947. The next year the Junior Welfare League of Rock Hill donated twenty-five hundred dollars and pledged one thousand dollars a year for five years. A board was organized and the York delegation gave fifteen thousand dollars. Mr. Dick Fewell donated land, with the stipulation that it would always be used for parks and playgrounds. The League oversaw construction of the building which was the first in the nation to be used solely as a children's nature museum.

The Children's Nature Museum opened on August 1, 1950. The director was a sustaining member until the arrival of J. Lee Settlemyre in 1952. In 1956 the museum was turned over to the county. The museum relocated in 1966 and the League hosted the formal opening.

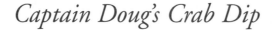

Captain Doug's Crab Dip

3 ounces lump crab meat	1 tablespoon curry powder
8 ounces cream cheese, softened	1/2 teaspoon Worcestershire sauce
2 tablespoons mayonnaise	2 tablespoons chopped onion
1 teaspoon lemon juice	Grated Parmesan cheese

- Combine the crab meat, cream cheese and mayonnaise in a bowl and mix well. Add the lemon juice, curry powder, Worcestershire sauce and chopped onion and mix well. Spoon into a shallow baking dish. Sprinkle with the Parmesan cheese. Bake at 400 degrees for 30 minutes. Serve with crackers.
- *Yield: 4 servings*

Hot Creamed Crab Dip

Mrs. Charles L. Okey, Jr. (Tina C.), Past President, 1948–1949

8 ounces cream cheese, softened	1 teaspoon flour
1/2 cup mayonnaise	Dash of pepper
4 1/2 teaspoons lemon juice	1 (7-ounce) can crab meat,
1/2 teaspoon Worcestershire sauce	drained, shredded

- Beat the cream cheese in a mixing bowl until smooth. Add the mayonnaise, lemon juice, Worcestershire sauce, flour and pepper and beat until smooth. Fold in the crab meat. Spoon into a baking dish.
- Bake, covered, at 300 degrees for 20 minutes. Serve with crackers.
- *Yield: 8 to 10 servings*

Thai Crab Dip

⅔ cup heavy cream
2 ounces shredded coconut
1 (6-ounce) can crab meat, drained
2 scallions, minced
1 tablespoon minced fresh cilantro
2 tablespoons lime juice
1 Thai chile, or ⅓ ancho chile, seeded, chopped
Salt to taste

- Combine the cream and coconut in a saucepan and bring to a boil. Remove from heat immediately. Let stand for 10 minutes, to infuse the flavor. Strain, reserving the coconut for another use. Let stand until cool.
- Combine the cooled cream, crab meat, scallions, cilantro, lime juice and Thai chile and mix well. Season with the salt. Chill, covered, in the refrigerator.
- Spoon into a serving bowl. Serve with unpeeled sliced cucumbers or red bell pepper strips.
- *Yield: 32 servings*

APPETIZERS

THE "WELL BABY STATION"

In 1940 the Junior Welfare League established a "Well Baby Station," where needy families could bring their children to be seen by a doctor. Also, they received food, clothing, fuel, layettes, and lots of milk. An average of twelve children a month were seen, and the "Well Baby Station" continued until 1947, when services became available at the local health department.

Hot Crawfish Dip

2 tablespoons butter
1/2 teaspoon Worcestershire sauce
1/4 cup chopped green onions
2 tablespoons chopped fresh
    parsley

1 pound crawfish meat
8 ounces cream cheese, softened
1/4 cup milk
Salt to taste
Cayenne pepper to taste

- Heat the butter in a large saucepan until melted. Add the Worcestershire sauce, green onions and parsley. Sauté for 2 minutes. Add the crawfish meat. Cook until the crawfish is opaque and cooked through. Add the cream cheese and milk. Cook until the cream cheese is melted and mixture is heated through, stirring frequently. Season with the salt and cayenne pepper.
- Spoon into a chafing dish. Serve with a French bread round.
- *Yield: 16 to 18 servings*

Hot Shrimp Dip

8 ounces cream cheese
1/4 cup mayonnaise
1 teaspoon grated onion
1 teaspoon mustard
1 teaspoon sugar
3 tablespoons sherry

8 ounces shrimp, peeled,
    deveined, cooked, or
    1 (4-ounce) can shrimp,
    drained
Dash of salt and garlic powder
1/2 cup sliced almonds

- Heat the cream cheese in the top of a double boiler over simmering water until melted. Combine the next 8 ingredients in a blender container and process until smooth. Add the melted cream cheese and process until blended. Pour into a soufflé dish. Sprinkle the almonds over the top. Bake at 325 degrees for 30 minutes.
- *Yield: 6 to 8 servings*

Hot Virginia Dip

Martha J. Williams, Past President, 1991–1992

16 ounces cream cheese, softened
1 cup sour cream
1 (5-ounce) jar dried beef
¼ cup milk
1 teaspoon garlic salt
4 teaspoons minced onions
2 tablespoons butter
1 cup pecans

- Combine the cream cheese, sour cream, dried beef, milk, garlic salt and onions in a bowl and mix well. Spoon into a baking dish.
- Heat the butter in a skillet until melted. Add the pecans and sauté. Spoon over the cream cheese layer.
- Bake at 350 degrees for 20 minutes. Serve warm with crackers.
- *Yield: 8 servings*

"COME SEE ME"

The first "Come See Me" steering committee was organized in 1962, with several League members as representatives. At the time of the third festival, interest in the spring event was dwindling. Big-name entertainment was too expensive for the CSM budget and the festival was about to be canceled.

When the League learned that "Come See Me" was folding, they volunteered to produce a "Follies" for the 1964 festival. This cost CSM nothing and the committee graciously accepted the league offer. "Follies" was a huge success and the Junior Welfare League was credited for saving "Come See Me."

Hummus

2 cups cooked garbanzo beans
²/₃ cup tahini
³/₄ cup lemon juice
5 garlic cloves, or to taste
1 teaspoon salt
2 tablespoons olive oil
  (optional)

1 (4-ounce) can chopped olives,
  drained
1 pound pita bread, cut into
  wedges

- Combine the beans, tahini, lemon juice, garlic and salt in a mixing bowl and beat until smooth. Spoon onto a serving plate. Make an indentation in the top of the hummus. Spoon the olive oil into the indentation. Sprinkle the olives over the hummus. Serve with the pita wedges.
- *Yield: 12 to 15 servings*

Kahlúa Fruit Dip

8 ounces cream cheese, softened
8 ounces nondairy whipped
  topping
³/₄ cup packed light brown sugar

¹/₃ cup Kahlúa
1 cup sour cream
1 (3-ounce) package unsalted
  chopped peanuts (optional)

- Combine the cream cheese and whipped topping in a bowl and mix until smooth. Add the brown sugar and Kahlúa and mix well. Stir in the sour cream. Chill, covered, in the refrigerator for 1 to 2 days for enhanced flavor.
- Spoon into a serving bowl. Sprinkle with the chopped peanuts. Serve with fresh fruit.
- *Yield: 20 to 25 servings*

Mushroom and Sour Cream Dip

3 tablespoons butter
1 pound mushrooms, sliced
1 large onion, chopped
2 tablespoons water
1 teaspoon salt
1 garlic clove, minced
$1/2$ teaspoon pepper
$1/4$ cup chopped fresh parsley, or 2 tablespoons dried parsley
1 cup sour cream

- Heat the butter in a skillet until melted. Add the mushrooms and onion. Sauté until tender. Stir in the water, salt, garlic, pepper and parsley. Cook until heated through. Add the sour cream and mix well.
- Spoon into a fondue pot. Serve warm with toast points.
- *Yield: 10 to 12 servings*

Raspberry Black Bean Dip

1 (15-ounce) can black beans
Salt and pepper to taste
$1/4$ purple onion, chopped
8 ounces cream cheese, softened
8 ounces raspberry salsa
Shredded Monterey Jack pepper cheese to taste

- Rinse, drain and pat dry the black beans. Mash the beans in a bowl. Season with salt and pepper. Stir in the purple onion. Spread over the bottom of a baking dish. Layer the cream cheese and salsa over the bean layer. Sprinkle enough Monterey Jack pepper cheese to cover the layers.
- Bake at 350 degrees until the cheese melts. Serve with blue chips or nacho chips.
- *Yield: 14 to 16 servings*

SIP AND SEE

The Sip and See has quickly become a Rock Hill tradition to honor Mother and welcome her newborn baby. Very much like a baby shower, light food and punch is served. What makes this event so special is that "baby" is present and welcomed by Mother's friends, southern style.

Citrus Wine Welcomer

Cheese Straws

Kahlúa Fruit Dip with Fresh Fruit Plate

Shrimp Deviled Eggs

Finger Sandwiches made with
    Vegetable Sandwich Spread

Luscious Lemon Drops

Vidalia Onion Dip

2 cups chopped Vidalia onions **2 cups mayonnaise**
2 cups shredded Swiss cheese

- Combine the onions, cheese and mayonnaise in a bowl and mix well. Spoon into a pie plate sprayed with nonstick cooking spray.
- Bake at 325 degrees for 25 minutes. Serve with crackers, crusty bread or apple slices.
- *Yield: 8 to 10 servings*

Vulture Dip

1 (10-ounce) package frozen chopped spinach, thawed **8 ounces cream cheese, softened**
1 cup diced canned tomatoes **1 teaspoon cumin**
1/2 cup picante sauce **2 cups grated Mexican 3- or 4-cheese blend**
1/4 cup chopped green onions

- Drain the spinach, pressing to remove excess moisture. Combine the spinach, tomatoes, picante sauce, green onions, cream cheese and cumin in a bowl and mix well. Fold in 3/4 cup of the cheese. Spoon into a shallow baking dish. Sprinkle the remaining 1 1/4 cups cheese over the top.
- Bake at 350 degrees for 30 minutes or until the cheese is hot and melted. You may microwave this dish. Serve with plain tortilla chips.
- *Yield: 20 servings*

Spinach and Cheese Torte

4 cups shredded sharp Cheddar cheese

$^1/_2$ cup chopped toasted pecans

$^1/_2$ cup mayonnaise

1 (10-ounce) package frozen chopped spinach, thawed

8 ounces cream cheese, softened

$^1/_4$ teaspoon salt

$^1/_2$ teaspoon freshly ground pepper

8 ounces cream cheese, softened

$^1/_4$ cup chutney

$^1/_4$ teaspoon nutmeg

Toasted chopped pecans for garnish

- Line a 5×9-inch loaf pan with plastic wrap. Combine the Cheddar cheese, pecans and mayonnaise in a bowl and mix well. Spread half of the mixture evenly over the bottom of the prepared pan.

- Drain the spinach, pressing to remove excess moisture. Combine the spinach, 8 ounces cream cheese, salt and pepper in a bowl and mix well. Spread evenly over the Cheddar cheese layer.

- Combine the remaining 8 ounces cream cheese, chutney and nutmeg in a bowl and mix well. Spread evenly over the spinach layer. Spread the remaining Cheddar cheese mixture evenly over the top.

- Chill, covered, until firm. Unmold onto a serving plate. Garnish with chopped toasted pecans. Serve with crackers. You may use light mayonnaise and cream cheese. You may freeze this torte for up to 1 month.

- *Yield: 1 loaf*

As was common in the days of old, most ladies regularly attended daytime bridge clubs, teas, and book clubs, where the food was often the main attraction. It was a time when women got dressed up just to go shopping and hats and gloves were a part of every outfit. The menus for these get-togethers usually consisted of chicken salad, cheese straws, toasted pecans, punch, and a lovely parfait dessert.

Bridge Club Punch

1 quart sweetened tea
1 quart orange juice
1 quart pineapple juice
$1/2$ cup lemon juice
Fruit slices for garnish
Maraschino cherries for garnish

- Combine the tea, orange juice, pineapple juice and lemon juice in a large bowl and mix well. Pour over ice in a punch bowl. Garnish with fruit slices and maraschino cherries.
- *Yield: 25 ($1/2$-cup) servings*

Citrus Wine Welcomer

2 cups orange juice
1 (6-ounce) can frozen lemonade concentrate, thawed
1 cup orange-flavored liqueur
1 (750-milliliter) bottle dry white wine, chilled
1 (1-liter) bottle club soda, chilled
Crushed ice
Orange slices for garnish

- Combine the orange juice, lemonade concentrate, liqueur and wine in a punch bowl and mix well. Add the club soda and crushed ice, stirring gently. Garnish with orange slices.
- *Yield: 22 ($1/2$-cup) servings*

Cranberry Slush

1 (32-ounce) bottle cranberry juice cocktail
1 (12-ounce) can frozen lemonade concentrate, thawed
1½ cups Kentucky bourbon
1 (28-ounce) bottle ginger ale

- Combine the cranberry juice cocktail, lemonade concentrate and bourbon in a freezer-safe container and mix well. Freeze until slushy. Spoon about ³/₄ cup of the cranberry mixture into each of 10 glasses. Pour about ¹/₄ cup of the ginger ale over the slush in each glass.
- *Yield: 10 (1-cup) servings*

Dreamsicle Punch

1 (14-ounce) can sweetened condensed milk
1 (46-ounce) can pineapple juice, chilled
1 (2-liter) bottle orange soda, chilled
Orange sherbet (optional)

- Combine the condensed milk and pineapple juice in a punch bowl and mix well. Stir in the soda. Place scoops of orange sherbet over the top.
- *Yield: 32 (¹/₂-cup) servings*

Holiday Shrub

1 (750-milliliter) bottle white port wine
1 (12-ounce) can frozen limeade concentrate, thawed
Juice of 1 lemon
1½ cups water
2 tablespoons sugar (optional)
Strawberries for garnish
Mint sprigs for garnish

- Combine the wine, limeade concentrate, lemon juice, water and sugar in a large plastic pitcher and mix well. Freeze, covered, for 8 to 12 hours. Place in the refrigerator for 15 minutes, stirring occasionally with a spoon to make slushy.
- Pour into old-fashioned glasses or large wine glasses. Garnish with strawberries and mint sprigs.
- *Yield: 8 (½-cup) servings*

Holly Punch

1 (6-ounce) can frozen orange juice concentrate, thawed
1 (6-ounce) can frozen lemonade concentrate, thawed
1 quart cranberry juice cocktail
1 quart ginger ale, chilled
1 orange, thinly sliced

- Combine the orange juice concentrate, lemonade concentrate and cranberry juice cocktail in a pitcher and mix well. Chill in the refrigerator. Stir in the ginger ale. Serve immediately. Garnish with orange slices.
- *Yield: 12 (6-ounce) servings*

MYCO's Champagne Punch

1 (750-milliliter) bottle champagne, chilled
1 quart club soda, chilled
1 quart ginger ale, chilled
1 cup cranberry juice cocktail, chilled

- Pour the champagne, club soda, ginger ale and cranberry juice over ice or an ice mold in a punch bowl and stir to mix. You may double or triple this.
- *Yield: 36 (¹/2-cup) servings*

Sherry Bolo

9 gallons sherry
8 (16-ounce) cans frozen pink lemonade concentrate, thawed
4 cups sugar
4 (3-liter) bottles lemon-lime soda
1 quart ginger ale
1 gallon apple juice (optional)

- Combine the sherry, lemonade concentrate, sugar, lemon-lime soda, ginger ale and apple juice in a very large container and mix well. Freeze, covered, until slushy.
- *Yield: 426 (¹/2-cup) servings*

BEVERAGES

PAST PRESIDENTS

My years as a League member prepared me for the many jobs I have had at the Museum of York County, from volunteer coordinator, to events coordinator, to fund raiser. We have served gallons of both of these "festive" punches at museum events.

— Mrs. W. C. Spencer (Ann A.)

Southern Comfort Punch

2½ cups Southern Comfort
¾ cup lemon juice
2 (6-ounce) cans frozen
  lemonade concentrate, thawed

2¼ liters lemon-lime soda,
  chilled
1 (4-ounce) jar maraschino
  cherries

- Combine the Southern Comfort, lemon juice and lemonade concentrate in a pitcher and mix well. Chill, covered, in the refrigerator. Pour into a punch bowl. Stir in the lemon-lime soda and cherries.
- *Yield: 13 (1-cup) servings*

Witches' Brew

4 cups apple cider
2 cups cranberry juice cocktail
½ cup orange juice
2 cups vodka
1 cup brandy

1 teaspoon whole allspice
1½ teaspoons whole cloves
2 cinnamon sticks
Cranberries (optional)

- Combine the apple cider, cranberry juice, orange juice, vodka, brandy, allspice, cloves and cinnamon sticks in a large container and mix well. Chill for 4 to 6 hours; strain. Pour into glasses and garnish with fresh cranberries.
- *Yield: 15 to 18 servings*

Brunch
& Breads

Untitled
Harriet Marshall Goode

Harriet Marshall Goode

In Harriet Marshall Goode's paintings of women, one can see the influence of her surroundings. The ordinary sights and sounds in the routine of daily life affect her, and when she travels to a foreign country or to a different region of this country, these influences create dramatic changes in her work.

Harriet Marshall Goode, affectionately known by most as "Sister," was born and raised in Rock Hill. She has painted since her early college days and has been a working artist for almost twenty years. Sister's work has won numerous honors and awards, and can be seen in private and corporate collections throughout the United States, Europe, China, Canada, and Mexico.

Betty Jo's Eggs Benedict Casserole

Mrs. J. C. Rhea, Jr. (Betty Jo Dunlap), Past President, 1958–1959

8 slices Canadian bacon
1 (8-ounce) package shredded Swiss cheese
8 eggs
1 cup (about) heavy cream
Grated Parmesan cheese
4 English muffins, split

- Arrange the Canadian bacon over the bottom of a 9×13-inch baking dish. Sprinkle the Swiss cheese over the bacon. Break the eggs evenly over the cheese. Drizzle enough of the cream over the eggs so that only the yolks show.
- Bake at 350 degrees for 10 minutes. Sprinkle Parmesan cheese over the top. Bake for an additional 8 to 10 minutes. Serve over the English muffins.
- *Yield: 8 servings*

PAST PRESIDENTS

I have used this recipe for a New Year's Eve late supper. It is great with a hot fruit casserole and toasted and buttered English muffins.

—Mrs. J. C. Rhea, Jr. (Betty Jo Dunlap)

Note: Betty Jo Rhea went on to become mayor of Rock Hill from 1986 to 1998. She will always be remembered by the public for preparing Rock Hill for the twenty-first century. She pushed for beautification projects and attracted many new businesses to the area. During her time as mayor, Betty Jo Rhea was rarely seen without an attractive scarf perfectly placed at her neckline.

Two pounds of bacon, sliced

Preheat the broiler. Place bacon in batches on a rack in the broiler pan. Broil for 1 to 2 minutes per side or until of the desired crispness. Drain well. May be packed in freezer bags and frozen or refrigerated. Microwave on a microwave-safe plate until heated through.

Eggs with Hollandaise

12 eggs	**Shredded cheese to taste**
Chopped green onions to taste	**Salt and pepper to taste**
1½ cups half-and-half	**1 envelope hollandaise sauce**

- Grease 12 muffin cups. Break 1 egg into each muffin cup. Sprinkle green onions over the eggs. Pour 2 tablespoons of the half-and-half into each muffin cup. Sprinkle cheese over the half-and-half. Season with salt and pepper. Bake at 300 degrees for 10 to 15 minutes or until the eggs are set.
- Prepare the hollandaise sauce using the package directions. Spoon evenly over the cooked eggs. Bake until heated through.
- *Yield: 6 to 12 servings*

Scrambled Eggs for a Crowd

2 tablespoons butter, softened	**Pinch of pepper**
12 eggs	**2 tablespoons heavy cream**
¼ teaspoon salt	

- Coat a cold skillet with the butter. Beat the eggs, salt and pepper in a mixing bowl until pale yellow. Pour the egg mixture into the prepared skillet. Cook over medium-low heat until the eggs thicken, stirring constantly. Cook until the eggs are of the desired consistency, stirring rapidly and constantly. Remove from the heat. Stir in the cream. Spoon into a serving bowl.
- *Yield: 8 servings*

Cheese Soufflé

¼ cup (½ stick) butter
¼ cup flour
1 cup milk
½ teaspoon salt
¼ teaspoon pepper

½ teaspoon dry mustard
1½ cups shredded
    Cheddar cheese
4 egg yolks
4 egg whites

- Heat the butter in a small saucepan until melted. Stir in the flour. Cook until well blended, stirring constantly. Add the milk, whisking constantly. Cook until the mixture is thick, stirring constantly. Add the salt, pepper, dry mustard and cheese and mix well. Remove from the heat. Let stand until slightly cooled. Beat the egg yolks in a mixing bowl until pale yellow. Stir a small amount of the cheese mixture into the egg yolks. Stir the egg yolks into the cheese mixture.
- Beat the egg whites in a mixing bowl until stiff. Fold in the cheese mixture. Spoon into a greased 1½-quart soufflé dish. Cover and freeze for 8 to 10 hours. Bake, uncovered, at 300 degrees for 1½ hours.
- *Yield: 6 servings*

Tomato Grits Casserole

1 pound hot sausage
1 cup grits
2 cups shredded sharp
    Cheddar cheese
4 eggs, beaten

1 (16-ounce) can diced
    tomatoes, drained
Pinch of salt
Pinch of pepper

- Cook the sausage in a skillet, stirring until crumbly; drain. Cook the grits in a large pot using the package directions. Remove from the heat. Add the cheese to the hot grits, stirring until melted. Stir in the sausage, eggs and tomatoes. Season with salt and pepper. Spoon into a greased baking dish. Bake at 350 degrees for 1 hour.
- *Yield: 6 servings*

Ham and Cheese Grits Casserole

1½ cups nonfat milk

2¼ cups water

1 teaspoon salt

1¼ cups quick-cooking grits

4 ounces cooked ham, diced (about ¾ cup)

3 ounces low-fat Monterey Jack cheese, shredded (about ¾ cup)

2 tablespoons grated Parmesan cheese

1 pickled jalapeño chile, minced

2 eggs

3 egg whites

2 cups nonfat milk

- Combine 1½ cups milk, water and salt in a saucepan. Bring to a boil over medium-high heat. Stir in the grits gradually, whisking constantly. Reduce the heat to low. Simmer, covered, for 5 minutes, stirring occasionally. Remove from the heat. Stir in the ham, Monterey Jack cheese, Parmesan cheese and jalapeño chile.
- Whisk the eggs, egg whites and 2 cups milk in a large bowl. Stir in the grits mixture gradually; the mixture will be lumpy.
- Spoon the grits mixture into a greased shallow 2-quart baking dish. Bake at 325 degrees for 45 to 50 minutes or until the top is set and the edges are golden brown. Let stand for 10 minutes.
- *Yield: 6 servings*

Martha's "Meant to Be" Cheese Danish

1 (8-count) package refrigerated crescent rolls
16 ounces cream cheese, softened
1 cup sugar
1 egg
1 teaspoon vanilla extract
1 (8-count) package refrigerated crescent rolls
$\frac{1}{2}$ cup (1 stick) butter or margarine, melted
$\frac{1}{2}$ cup sugar
1 teaspoon cinnamon
1 cup chopped pecans

- Preheat oven to 350 degrees. Unroll 1 package crescent rolls. Press over the bottom and slightly up the sides of a greased 9×13-inch baking dish, pressing the perforations to seal.
- Combine the cream cheese, 1 cup sugar, egg and vanilla in a bowl and mix well. Spread over the dough.
- Unroll 1 package crescent rolls. Arrange over the cream cheese layer, pressing the perforations to seal.
- Combine the butter, $\frac{1}{2}$ cup sugar, cinnamon and pecans in a bowl and mix well. Spread evenly over the top. Bake for 30 minutes or until golden brown.
- *Yield: 16 servings*

"MEANT TO BE"

Martha Cranford's mother, a southern lady from Mississippi, called her loving daughter for a recipe to serve her bridge club the next day. The recipe had to be simple because Mother did not have a lot of time. Martha gave her mother this delicious recipe and mentioned in the conversation that these pastries were "meant to be" for her bridge club. Mother called Martha the next evening and, assuming this was the name of the recipe, raved about her "meant to be" Danish. They had quite a laugh, and hence, the name.

Scones

4¹/₂ cups sifted flour
2 teaspoons baking powder
¹/₂ teaspoon baking soda
2 tablespoons sugar
Pinch of salt
1 cup (2 sticks) butter, cut into small pieces
1 to 1¹/₄ cups heavy cream
1 egg
¹/₄ cup light cream

- Preheat oven to 375 degrees. Sift the flour, baking powder, baking soda, sugar and salt into a large bowl. Cut in the butter until crumbly. You may process half the flour mixture with the butter in a food processor container and stir in the remaining flour mixture.
- Stir in enough of the heavy cream for the mixture to hold together. Chill, wrapped in plastic wrap, for 30 minutes. Roll into a ¹/₂-inch-thick circle for small scones and a ¹/₄-inch-thick circle for large scones on a lightly floured surface. Cut the dough into the desired shapes.
- Place the scones on a buttered baking sheet. Combine the egg and light cream in a bowl and mix well. Brush over the tops of the scones. Bake for 13 to 15 minutes or until golden brown and puffed. Serve with jellies.
- For **Savory Scones,** add ¹/₄ cup caraway seeds, ¹/₄ cup poppy seeds or ¹/₄ cup finely chopped dill to the dough before adding the cream.
- For **Sweet Scones,** add ¹/₄ cup minced candied orange peel or 1 cup currants soaked in 3 tablespoons brandy.
- *Yield: 40 (1-inch) scones*

Angel Biscuits

1 envelope dry yeast	1½ teaspoons salt
3 tablespoons warm water	1 teaspoon baking soda
5 cups flour	1 cup shortening
1 tablespoon baking powder	2 cups buttermilk
5 tablespoons sugar	Crème Fraîche

- Dissolve the yeast in the warm water in a small bowl. Sift the flour, baking powder, sugar, salt and baking soda into a large bowl. Cut in the shortening until crumbly. Add the yeast mixture and buttermilk and mix well. Knead on a lightly floured surface. Divide the dough into two equal portions. Chill, covered, for up to 10 days.
- Roll the dough ½ inch thick on a lightly floured surface. Cut with a biscuit cutter. Place the biscuits on a baking sheet. Let stand until room temperature. Bake at 400 degrees for 15 minutes or until light brown. Serve with Crème Fraîche.
- *Yield: 30 biscuits*

Crème Fraîche

2 cups heavy cream
2 tablespoons buttermilk or sour cream

- Heat the cream in a saucepan to 100 degrees. Add the buttermilk and mix well. Pour into a jar with a tight-fitting lid and seal tightly. Let stand at room temperature for 6 to 8 hours. Chill in the refrigerator for 24 hours or longer.

BRUNCH & BREADS

ANGEL BISCUITS

Those who have eaten Addie Mayfield's Angel Biscuits say they are so light they could float right up to the pearly gates. Mrs. Mayfield said the secret is in sifting the flour. "There are always a few lumps that won't go through the sifter. These should be discarded." Another secret is to dissolve the yeast in warm water and let it stand for about an hour. Serve these Angel Biscuits to your family and you just might be considered a "Saint."

I inherited my beaten biscuit machine from my grandmother, making it well over one hundred and fifty years old. The special dough is fed through two rollers powered by the strength of arm muscles. The boys of each generation are given the privilege of turning the "crank" to develop strong muscles. This whole operation is truly a labor of love and shared only with people who appreciate the biscuits. These are so special that they are usually made for big family Christmas dinners, parties, or receptions. Now, with our family scattered, I try to send some to Pennsylvania, Kentucky, Tennessee, Texas, and Florida, as well as the Carolinas.

—Mrs. R. H. Mackintosh
(Mary Elizabeth Fewell)

Beaten Biscuits

Mrs. R. H. Mackintosh (Mary Elizabeth Fewell), Past President, 1960–1961

4 cups flour, sifted
2 teaspoons sugar
1 teaspoon salt
1 teaspoon (heaping) baking powder
1/2 cup shortening or lard
1/2 cup milk
1/2 cup ice water

- Combine the flour, sugar, salt and baking powder in a bowl and mix well. Cut in the shortening until crumbly. Combine the milk and ice water in a bowl. Stir into the flour mixture; the mixture will be stiff.
- Run the dough through a biscuit-beating machine 75 times or until it is a smooth ribbon that blisters and pops on the board. You may beat by hand on a floured surface using a 2-pound wooden mallet. Cut with a small sharp biscuit cutter. Prick each biscuit with a fork. Place on a baking sheet.
- Bake at 350 degrees for 25 to 30 minutes; do not allow to brown. Serve hot with melted butter or a sliver of country ham. You may freeze the biscuits.
- *Yield: 2 dozen*

Sour Cream Tiny Biscuits

½ cup (1 stick) butter, softened
½ cup (1 stick) margarine, softened
2 cups self-rising flour
1 cup fat-free sour cream

- Combine the butter, margarine and flour in a bowl and mix well. Stir in the sour cream. Drop 1½ teaspoons into each of 36 greased miniature muffin cups. Bake at 350 degrees for 20 to 25 minutes.
- *Yield: 3 dozen*

Cheese Muffins

Mrs. Pride Ratteree, Jr. (Gwen), Past President, 1946–1947

2 cups baking mix
1 cup shredded cheese
1 cup sour cream
½ cup (1 stick) butter, melted

- Combine the baking mix, cheese, sour cream and butter in a bowl and mix well. Fill 12 greased muffin cups almost to the top. Bake at 400 degrees for 15 minutes.
- *Yield: 1 dozen*

Contrast is the secret of attractive meals:

Flavor Contrast: Balance a spicy dish with a cool salad or a mildly flavored dessert.

Color Contrast: Visualize how the food will look on the plate. Avoid using a yellow rice and yellow vegetable at the same time. Add a bright garnish or vegetable if needed.

Texture Contrast: Serve something crisp with something soft; combine smooth with chewy, dry with moist.

Shape Contrast: Cut vegetables different ways depending on the other foods you are serving. For example, penne pasta with round-cut vegetables or rice with diagonally cut pieces.

Temperature Contrast: Serve a hot soup with a chilled salad, hot pasta with icy sherbet.

Mexican Corn Muffins

1 cup yellow cornmeal
1 cup flour
1 tablespoon sugar
1 teaspoon baking powder
2 egg whites, lightly beaten
1 cup buttermilk
$1/4$ cup unsweetened applesauce
1 (4-ounce) can diced green chile peppers, drained
$3/4$ cup finely shredded reduced-fat sharp Cheddar cheese

- Combine the cornmeal, flour, sugar and baking powder in a large bowl and mix well. Make a well in the center.
- Combine the egg whites, buttermilk and applesauce in a bowl and mix well. Pour into the well in the cornmeal mixture. Stir just until moistened. Fold in the chile peppers and $1/2$ cup of the cheese.
- Fill twelve $2^1/2$-inch muffin cups sprayed with nonstick cooking spray $3/4$ full. Sprinkle the remaining $1/4$ cup cheese over the tops. Bake at 400 degrees for 14 to 16 minutes or until golden brown and a wooden pick inserted in the center comes out clean. Cool in the pan for 5 minutes. Remove to a wire rack to cool completely.
- *Yield: 1 dozen*

Blueberry Bread

3 cups cake flour

2 teaspoons baking powder

1/2 teaspoon salt

1 1/2 cups sugar

3 tablespoons plus

   2 teaspoons margarine

1 cup milk

1 tablespoon vanilla extract

1 egg, lightly beaten

1 1/2 cups fresh blueberries

Almond Topping

- Combine the cake flour, baking powder, salt and sugar in a large bowl and mix well. Cut in the margarine until crumbly. Combine the milk, vanilla and egg in a small bowl and mix well. Pour into the dry ingredients. Stir just until moistened; the batter will be lumpy. Stir in the blueberries gently.
- Spoon into a 5×9-inch loaf pan sprayed with nonstick cooking spray. Sprinkle the Almond Topping evenly over the batter.
- Bake at 350 degrees for 1 hour and 20 minutes or until a wooden pick inserted in the center comes out clean. Cool in the pan for 10 minutes. Remove to a wire rack to cool completely.
- *Yield: 1 loaf*

Almond Topping

2 tablespoons cake flour

2 tablespoons sugar

1/2 teaspoon cinnamon

1 teaspoon margarine

1 tablespoon chopped

   almonds

- Combine the cake flour, sugar and cinnamon in a bowl and mix well. Cut in the margarine until crumbly. Stir in the almonds.

ORTHOPEDIC AND THERAPY SCHOOL

In 1951 the League house on West Main Street became the home for a crippled children's school called the Orthopedic and Therapy School. There was one teacher and a physiotherapist. Members assisted with the children in many ways and gave thousands of dollars for funding. Some League members taught music and typing lessons. The school remained at the League house until 1969.

Pumpkin Bread

3 cups sugar

1 cup vegetable oil

3 eggs

2 cups canned pumpkin

3 cups flour

1/2 teaspoon salt

1/2 teaspoon baking powder

1 teaspoon cinnamon

1 teaspoon nutmeg

1 teaspoon baking soda

- Combine the sugar, oil and eggs in a bowl and mix well. Add the pumpkin, flour, salt, baking powder, cinnamon, nutmeg and baking soda and mix well. Pour into two 5×9-inch loaf pans.
- Bake at 350 degrees for 45 minutes.
- *Yield: 2 loaves*

Sour Cream Rolls

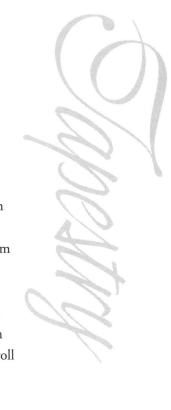

½ cup (1 stick) butter or margarine

1 cup sour cream

½ cup sugar

2 envelopes dry yeast

½ cup warm (105- to 115-degree) water

2 eggs, beaten

4 cups flour

1 teaspoon salt

Melted butter or margarine

- Bring ½ cup butter to a boil in a saucepan. Remove from the heat. Stir in the sour cream and sugar. Let stand until lukewarm.
- Dissolve the yeast in the warm water in a large bowl. Stir in the sour cream mixture and the eggs. Add the flour and salt gradually, mixing well after each addition. Chill, covered, for 8 to 12 hours.
- Divide the dough into 4 equal portions. Roll each portion into a 10-inch circle on a lightly floured surface. Brush with the melted butter. Cut each circle into 12 wedges. Roll up the wedges from the wide ends. You may roll the dough ⅓-inch thick and cut with a round biscuit cutter. Brush the rolls with the melted butter. Fold each roll over.
- Place the rolls on a greased baking sheet. Let rise, covered, for 1 hour or until doubled in bulk. Bake at 375 degrees for 10 minutes.
- *Yield: 4 dozen*

Mother's Yeast Rolls

Mrs. John A. Johnson (Carolyn Meyer), Past President, 1964–1965

4 cups flour
1 tablespoon salt
2 cups milk
$1/2$ cup shortening
$1/2$ cup sugar
$1/4$ cup warm water
1 tablespoon sugar
2 envelopes dry yeast

- Sift the flour and salt together. Scald the milk in a saucepan; do not boil. Remove from the heat. Add the shortening and $1/2$ cup sugar to the hot milk, stirring until dissolved. Cool to lukewarm.
- Combine the warm water and 1 tablespoon sugar in a bowl. Dissolve the yeast in the sugar water. Add the lukewarm milk mixture. Stir in the flour mixture. Place in a greased bowl, turning to coat the surface. Let rise, covered, in a warm place for 1 hour or until doubled in bulk. Punch the dough down. Refrigerate, covered, for 3 hours or longer.
- Roll the dough $1/4$ inch thick on a lightly floured surface. Cut with a biscuit cutter. You may dip the biscuits in butter and fold for pocketbook rolls. Arrange on a greased baking sheet. Let rise, covered, for $1 1/2$ hours or until doubled in bulk.
- Preheat oven to 325 degrees. Bake for 15 minutes on the lower oven rack. Bake for an additional 10 minutes on the top oven rack. You may freeze the rolls but do not allow them to brown as much.
- *Yield: 6 dozen*

Yeast Rolls

1 cup margarine, butter or shortening, softened
1 tablespoon salt
1/2 cup sugar
1 cup water
2 envelopes dry yeast
1 cup warm water
2 eggs, lightly beaten
6 cups bread flour

- Combine the margarine, salt and sugar in a large bowl and mix well. Bring 1 cup water to a boil in a saucepan. Pour over the margarine mixture.
- Dissolve the yeast in 1 cup warm water in a bowl. Let stand for 10 minutes. Stir into the margarine mixture. Add the eggs and mix well. Add the flour gradually, mixing well after each addition; the dough will be sticky. Place in a greased bowl, turning to coat the surface. Chill, covered, for 8 to 12 hours. Punch the dough down.
- Roll the dough on a lightly floured surface. Cut with a round biscuit cutter. Fold each roll over, pinching the edges to seal. Arrange on a greased baking sheet; the rolls should be just touching each other. Let rise for 1 hour or until doubled in bulk.
- Bake at 350 degrees for 10 minutes or until light brown. You may freeze the rolls.
- *Yield: 8 dozen*

Cheesy French Bread

1 (16-ounce) loaf French bread
1 (8-ounce) package shredded Mexican cheese
$^3/_4$ cup mayonnaise
1$^1/_2$ teaspoons parsley
$^1/_8$ teaspoon garlic powder

- Cut the bread into halves lengthwise. Combine the cheese, mayonnaise, parsley and garlic powder in a bowl and mix well. Spread over the cut sides of the bread. Place on a baking sheet.
- Bake at 350 degrees for 15 to 20 minutes or until light brown.
- *Yield: 6 to 8 servings*

Bread Bowls

1 (16-ounce) loaf frozen white bread dough, thawed

- Place four 2$^1/_2$×5-inch ovenproof bowls on a baking sheet. Grease the outside of each bowl.
- Divide the dough into 4 equal portions. Roll each portion into a circle on a lightly floured surface. Stretch each circle over a bowl. Let stand, covered, for 20 minutes.
- Preheat the oven to 375 degrees. Bake for 25 to 30 minutes or until light brown. Remove the bowls and set the bread bowls right side up on the baking sheet. Bake for an additional 5 to 7 minutes or until golden brown on the inside. Cool for 10 minutes.
- Fill bowls with chili topped with Cheddar cheese and green onions or with other filling of choice.
- *Yield: 4 servings*

Wisteria Balustrade
Sybil Mitchell

Soups
& Salads

Sybil Mitchell

Sybil Mitchell's painting is titled Wisteria Balustrade. *Her subject choices are triggered from an emotional response, in which she expresses her personal feelings and interpretations based on experiences, making her paintings more than just a record.*

Sybil Mitchell, a Rock Hill area resident, has been painting for more than twenty years. Sybil has won numerous honors, which include awards in exhibitions throughout the Southeast, and is a member of many professional associations and organizations.

Venison Chili

1/4 pound salt pork, cut into 4 pieces	2 or 3 large green chiles, chopped
2 pounds ground venison	1 garlic clove, minced
2 medium onions, chopped	3 tablespoons chili powder
1 (14-ounce) can diced tomatoes	3/4 teaspoon oregano
1 cup water	1/2 teaspoon cumin seeds, crushed
3/4 cup red wine	

- Brown the salt pork in a Dutch oven over medium heat. Add the venison and onions. Cook over medium-high heat until the venison is brown, stirring until crumbly; drain. Add the undrained tomatoes, water, wine, green chiles, garlic, chili powder, oregano and cumin seeds. Reduce the heat. Simmer for 1 hour, stirring occasionally. Remove the salt pork.
- *Yield: 7 servings*

Chicken Chowder

Mrs. T. Thomas (Mary Frances), Past President, 1972–1973

4 chicken breast halves	6 medium carrots, sliced
4 cups water	3 medium onions, chopped
1 teaspoon salt	1 (10-ounce) package frozen green peas
1/4 teaspoon pepper	
3 large potatoes, cubed	1 (13-ounce) can evaporated milk

- Combine the chicken, water, salt and pepper in a large saucepan. Cook until the chicken is tender. Skim the top. Add the potatoes, carrots and onions. Bring to a boil. Reduce the heat. Simmer for 15 minutes or until the vegetables are tender. Remove the chicken. Cut into bite-size pieces, discarding the skin and bones. Return the chicken to the saucepan. Add the peas. Cook for 5 minutes. Stir in the evaporated milk. Adjust the seasonings. Cook until heated through; do not boil.
- *Yield: 6 servings*

SOUPS & SALADS

PAST PRESIDENTS

I left Rock Hill twelve years ago, and every time I use a recipe given to me by a friend, I fondly remember good times. My recipe box is like a journal of old friends!

I walk every morning with some friends, and we have recently commented about how food has changed in the last few years. No longer do you go to a cocktail party and have sausage balls and Fritos.

—Mrs. T. Thomas (Mary Frances)

63

Mark's Chicken Taco Soup

Mrs. Robert H. Hopkins (Cathie Carrouthers), Past President, 1983–1984

2 whole boneless chicken breasts
4 (10-ounce) cans chicken broth
1 medium onion, chopped
1 small green bell pepper, chopped
1 teaspoon minced garlic
1 (15-ounce) can diced tomatoes
1 (10-ounce) can tomatoes with green chiles
1 (15-ounce) can black beans, drained
1 (15-ounce) can cream-style corn
1 envelope taco seasoning mix
1 envelope ranch dressing mix
1/2 teaspoon cumin
Crumbled tortilla chips for garnish
Sour cream for garnish
Shredded lettuce for garnish

- Combine the chicken with enough water to cover in a saucepan. Bring to a boil. Boil until tender; drain. Cut the chicken into bite-size pieces.
- Combine the chicken broth, onion, bell pepper, garlic, tomatoes, tomatoes with green chiles, black beans, corn, taco seasoning mix, ranch dressing mix, cumin and chicken pieces in a large pot. Cook, covered, over low heat for 1 1/2 hours. Ladle into soup bowls. Top with crumbled tortilla chips, a dollop of sour cream and shredded lettuce. You may chill the soup, covered, for 1 day for enhanced flavor and reheat before serving.
- *Yield: 6 servings*

Shrimp Bisque

Mrs. C. Weldon Burns, Jr. (Rebecca Sellers), Past President, 1968–1969

3 tablespoons butter
$1/4$ cup flour
1 teaspoon salt
$1/4$ teaspoon pepper
1 medium onion, finely chopped
3 cups milk

1 cup bouillon
8 ounces shrimp, finely chopped
Chopped fresh parsley or dried
    parsley to taste
$1/2$ cup heavy cream
$1/4$ to $1/2$ cup dry sherry

- Heat the butter in a saucepan until melted. Stir in the flour, salt, pepper and onion. Add the milk and bouillon, whisking constantly. Cook until thickened, stirring constantly. You may prepare this in advance.
- Add the shrimp and parsley. Simmer for 20 minutes. Stir in the cream and sherry. Cook until heated through. You may substitute lobster or crab for the shrimp.
- *Yield: 4 servings*

Salmon Bisque

1 (10-ounce) can chicken broth
1 (8-ounce) can Alaska pink salmon
1 (10-ounce) jar mild chunky salsa
$1/2$ cup nonfat dill dip
Sour cream for garnish
Lemon twists for garnish

- Chill the broth and skim the top. Drain the salmon, removing the skin and excess fat. Combine the broth, salmon, salsa and dill dip in a food processor container. Process until mixed; do not purée.
- Ladle into soup bowls. Garnish with a dollop of sour cream and a lemon twist. You may serve this hot or cold.
- *Yield: 4 servings*

THE SPEECH AND HEARING CENTER

The Junior Welfare League of Rock Hill was approached in 1971 to help establish a speech and hearing center in Rock Hill. After finding a building on Oakland Avenue, members painted walls, made curtains, located furniture, and decorated the building for its opening in 1972. Members served placements as receptionists and had other general responsibilities.

When the center outgrew their home, the League pledged ten thousand dollars for a new building. The center first moved to a small building on Charlotte Avenue, then in 1990 to its present site on Ebenezer Road. A League member still serves on the Speech and Hearing Center board.

Black and White Soup

2 cups black beans	**3 tablespoons butter**
1 cube salt pork	**2 tablespoons flour**
1/2 cup chopped onion	**2 (10-ounce) cans cream of**
1 cup chopped celery	**celery soup**
1/2 cup chopped carrots	**2 (10-ounce) cans beef**
1 garlic clove, minced	**consommé**
1 teaspoon sugar	**2 1/2 cups milk**
1/4 teaspoon thyme	**1 cup shredded Cheddar cheese**
Dash of cayenne or red pepper	**1/2 teaspoon Worcestershire sauce**

- Sort and rinse the black beans. Combine with enough cold water to cover in a large saucepan. Bring to a boil. Boil for 2 minutes. Remove from the heat. Let stand, tightly covered, for 1 hour. Drain, reserving the liquid.
- Add enough water to the reserved liquid to measure 10 cups. Pour into a large saucepan. Add the beans, salt pork, onion, celery and carrots. Cook, covered, for 2 to 3 hours or until the beans are tender. Remove the beans, onion, celery and carrots and place in a blender container. Purée with a small amount of the hot liquid. Pour the puréed mixture into the hot liquid. Simmer, covered, for 30 minutes. Remove the salt pork. Strain the soup. Add the garlic, sugar, thyme and cayenne pepper. Chill and skim the soup.
- Melt the butter in a large saucepan. Stir in the flour until blended. Add the black soup gradually, whisking constantly. Bring to a boil. Remove from the heat and keep warm.
- Combine the celery soup, beef consommé, milk, cheese and Worcestershire sauce in a large saucepan. Cook over low heat until the cheese is melted and the white soup is heated through, stirring constantly; do not boil.
- Ladle 1/2 cup of the black soup and 1/2 cup of the white soup at the same time into a soup bowl. Repeat the process with remaining soup.
- *Yield: 10 servings*

Crowd-Pleasing Potato Soup

Mrs. Robert Carter Langston (Cynthia Hyatt), Past President, 1992–1993

1 to 2 tablespoons butter or margarine
1 large onion, chopped
5 to 10 pounds potatoes, peeled, cubed
2 chicken bouillon cubes
4 to 6 cups water
8 ounces cream cheese, softened, cut into pieces
Milk (optional)
Shredded sharp Cheddar cheese for garnish
Bacon, crisp-cooked, crumbled, for garnish
Chopped green vegetable of choice for garnish

- Heat the butter in a large saucepan until melted. Add the onion. Sauté until tender. Add the potatoes, bouillon cubes and enough water to cover the potatoes. Bring to a boil.
- Cook for 20 to 25 minutes or until the potatoes are tender. Mash the potatoes in the saucepan. Add the cream cheese. Cook until the cream cheese is melted, stirring constantly. Add enough milk to make of the desired consistency.
- Ladle into soup bowls. Garnish with Cheddar cheese, bacon and green vegetable.
- *Yield: Variable*

PAST PRESIDENTS

Potato soup is the recipe my family asked me to submit because it is their favorite. They like to eat this soup very thick with lots of sharp Cheddar sprinkled on top. The standard menu is the soup, a large salad, and garlic bread or sour cream corn muffins.

—Mrs. Robert Carter Langston
(Cynthia Hyatt)

*Perhaps the most notable
accomplishment of the Junior
Welfare League the year
I was president was the
establishment of the Fine Arts
Association, now known as
ARTS etc. It began as a
League project in the Civic
and Cultural Committee
with Jeannine Burger,
chair, and with a concert
performance by the Charlotte
Symphony.*

—Mrs. Martin Goode (Harriet Marshall)

Spinach Soup

Mrs. Martin Goode (Harriet Marshall), Past President, 1975–1976

2 (10-ounce) packages frozen
   chopped spinach, thawed
8 ounces cream cheese
½ cup (1 stick) butter
1 (14-ounce) can artichoke
   hearts, chopped
2 (10-ounce) cans chicken broth

1 tablespoon (or more)
   lemon juice
Nutmeg to taste
Salt and pepper to taste
1 lemon, thinly sliced, for
   garnish

- Combine the first 6 ingredients in a large saucepan. Heat over low heat until the cream cheese is melted, stirring constantly. Simmer for 30 minutes, stirring occasionally. Season with nutmeg, salt and pepper.
- Ladle into soup bowls. Garnish with lemon and a sprinkle of nutmeg.
- *Yield: 4 servings*

Tomato Bisque

Mrs. Charles B. Burnette III (Marcia Hagan), Past President, 1994–1995

2 large onions, chopped
5 large garlic cloves, minced
¼ cup (½ stick) butter
1 (28-ounce) can diced tomatoes
1 (46-ounce) can tomato juice
3 bay leaves

1 teaspoon each basil, dill,
   thyme and parsley
1 teaspoon baking soda
8 ounces cream cheese, softened,
   cut into pieces
2 cups light cream

- Combine the onions, garlic, butter, tomatoes, tomato juice and herbs in a large saucepan. Bring to a simmer. Simmer for 20 minutes, stirring occasionally. Stir in the baking soda. Simmer for 10 to 15 minutes. Add the cream cheese and light cream. Cook for 15 minutes, stirring frequently. Remove the bay leaves. Ladle into soup bowls.
- *Yield: 10 to 12 servings*

Bean Salad

1 (16-ounce) can green peas, drained
1 (16-ounce) can green beans, drained
1 heart of celery (4 or 5 inner ribs), chopped
1 large onion, chopped
1 (2-ounce) jar chopped pimentos
Salt and pepper to taste
Vinegar Salad Dressing

- Combine the peas, green beans, celery, onion and pimentos in a bowl and mix well. Season with salt and pepper. Pour the Vinegar Salad Dressing over the bean mixture. Marinate, covered, for 8 to 12 hours; drain. Spoon into a serving bowl.
- *Yield: 6 to 8 servings*

Vinegar Salad Dressing

1/3 cup salad oil
1/2 cup sugar
3/4 cup white vinegar
3/4 cup water

- Combine the salad oil, sugar, vinegar and water in a bowl and mix well.

PAST PRESIDENTS

Tomato Bisque is great served on a chilly day at a tailgate party! One of my Charlotte League friends shared this with me.

—Mrs. Charles B. Burnette III
(Marcia Hagan)

Napa Salad

Mrs. Don P. Ferguson, Sr. (Phyllis Taylor), Past President, 1978–1979

½ cup (1 stick) butter

½ cup sesame seeds

1 (2-ounce) package slivered
   almonds

2 (3-ounce) packages ramen
   noodles, crumbled

1 head Napa cabbage, chopped

5 green onions, chopped

½ cup vegetable oil

½ cup sugar

1 teaspoon soy sauce

¼ cup vinegar

¼ teaspoon salt

- Melt the butter in a skillet. Add the sesame seeds, almonds and ramen noodles, reserving the seasoning packets for another use. Cook until brown, stirring constantly. Chill, covered, in the refrigerator. Mix the noodle mixture, cabbage and green onions in a large bowl. Mix the remaining ingredients in a small bowl. Pour over the cabbage mixture and toss to coat.
- *Yield: 8 to 10 servings*

Marinated Mushroom Salad

Mrs. L. Loyd Ardrey (Barbara Brewer), Past President, 1988–1989

4½ tablespoons Dijon mustard

4½ tablespoons red wine vinegar

½ teaspoon each tarragon, salt
   and oregano

¼ teaspoon pepper

¾ cup salad oil

1 pound fresh mushrooms, sliced

Boston lettuce

- Combine the mustard and vinegar in a bowl and mix well. Add the tarragon, salt, oregano and pepper and mix well. Add the oil, whisking constantly. Layer the mushrooms in a flat dish. Pour the salad oil mixture over the mushrooms, covering completely. Marinate, covered, in the refrigerator for 2 to 3 hours; drain. Arrange the lettuce on a serving plate. Arrange the mushrooms over the lettuce. Garnish as desired.
- *Yield: 6 to 8 servings*

Marinated Black Olives and Cherry Tomatoes

1 cup vegetable oil

1 cup cider vinegar

2 teaspoons salt

1/4 teaspoon sugar

1 teaspoon cracked black pepper

1 teaspoon oregano

1 medium garlic clove, minced

1 pint cherry tomatoes

2 (8-ounce) cans pitted black olives, drained

- Combine the oil, vinegar, salt, sugar, pepper, oregano and garlic in a bowl and mix well. Pierce each tomato with a fork and place in a bowl. Add the olives. Pour the vinegar mixture over the tomatoes and olives. Marinate, covered, in the refrigerator for 4 hours or longer, stirring occasionally; drain.
- *Yield: 8 servings*

Tomato and Green Bean Salad

2 pounds fresh green beans, snapped

8 large tomatoes

3/4 cup kalamata olives, pitted

1/4 cup chopped green onions

1/4 cup chopped fresh basil

8 ounces feta cheese, crumbled

1/2 cup olive oil

3 tablespoons white wine vinegar

1 teaspoon salt

2 teaspoons pepper

- Bring enough water to cover the green beans to a boil in a saucepan. Add the green beans. Cook for 5 to 6 minutes or until tender-crisp; drain. Rinse with cold water; drain. Place in a large bowl.
- Cut the tomatoes into wedges. Add the tomatoes, olives, green onions, basil and feta cheese to the green beans.
- Whisk the olive oil, vinegar, salt and pepper in a bowl. Pour over the vegetable mixture and toss gently. Chill, covered, in the refrigerator.
- *Yield: 12 servings*

Grape Tomato Salad

1 (6-ounce) package portobello mushroom caps
1 tablespoon olive oil
1 small zucchini, cut into ½-inch pieces (about 1 cup)
1 small yellow squash, cut into ½-inch pieces (about 1 cup)
1 tablespoon olive oil
1 pint grape tomatoes, cut into halves
1 tablespoon olive oil
2 tablespoons chopped fresh basil
2 teaspoons grated Parmesan cheese
1 teaspoon finely minced garlic
Coarse salt to taste

• Rinse and dry the mushroom caps. Place in a bowl. Drizzle with
  1 tablespoon olive oil, rubbing to coat. Combine the zucchini and yellow
  squash in a separate bowl. Drizzle with 1 tablespoon olive oil and toss to
  coat. Thread on skewers. Grill the squash and mushrooms over medium-
  hot coals until golden brown and tender, turning occasionally. Let stand
  until cool.

• Cut the mushrooms into ½-inch pieces and place into a serving bowl.
  Remove the yellow squash and zucchini from the skewers and add to the
  mushrooms. Add the grape tomatoes. Drizzle with 1 tablespoon olive oil
  and toss to combine. Add the basil, cheese, garlic and salt and toss to
  combine. Serve at room temperature.

• *Yield: 4 to 6 servings*

Macaroni Salad

Mrs. Carlisle Clarke Moore III (Kathy Unger), Past President, 1999–2000

PAST PRESIDENTS

2 cups elbow macaroni	2 or 3 tomatoes, chopped
2 cups mayonnaise	¹/₂ cup chopped cucumber
2 teaspoons wine vinegar	¹/₄ cup chopped green bell pepper
2 garlic cloves, mashed	2 tablespoons chopped scallions
1 teaspoon salt	2 tablespoons prepared
Dash of pepper	horseradish

- Cook the macaroni using the package directions; drain. Rinse with cold water; drain. Combine the macaroni, mayonnaise, vinegar, garlic, salt, pepper, tomatoes, cucumber, bell pepper, scallions and horseradish in a large bowl and mix well. Chill, covered, for 8 to 12 hours. Adjust the seasonings. You may use low-fat mayonnaise.
- *Yield: 8 servings*

I would say that macaroni salad is my favorite family recipe, because every time we have it, it seems like we are celebrating a holiday— like the Fourth of July, Labor Day, or Memorial Day—or are having a picnic to get together with friends.

—Mrs. Carlisle Clark Moore III
(Kathy Unger)

Curried Rice Salad

1 cup rice	¹/₄ cup chopped green olives
2 cups chicken broth	1 (2-ounce) can sliced black
1 (6-ounce) jar marinated	olives (optional)
artichoke hearts	¹/₄ cup chopped green onions
¹/₄ to ¹/₂ teaspoon curry powder	¹/₄ cup chopped green bell
¹/₃ cup mayonnaise	pepper

- Cook the rice using the package directions and substituting the broth for the water. Let stand until cool.
- Drain the artichokes, reserving the marinade. Chop the artichokes. Mix the reserved marinade, curry powder and mayonnaise in a bowl.
- Combine the cooled rice, artichokes, olives, green onions and bell pepper in a bowl and mix well. Add the mayonnaise mixture and mix well. Chill, covered, in the refrigerator.
- *Yield: 6 to 8 servings*

Antipasto Salad

1 (16-ounce) package rotini
1 (15-ounce) can garbanzo beans, rinsed, drained
1 (3-ounce) package sliced pepperoni, cut into halves
1 (2-ounce) can sliced olives, drained
$\frac{1}{2}$ cup chopped red bell pepper
$\frac{1}{2}$ cup chopped green bell pepper
4 medium fresh mushrooms, sliced
2 garlic cloves, minced
2 tablespoons minced fresh basil, or 2 teaspoons dried basil
$1\frac{1}{2}$ teaspoons minced fresh oregano, or $\frac{1}{2}$ teaspoon dried oregano
2 teaspoons salt
$\frac{1}{2}$ teaspoon black pepper
$\frac{1}{4}$ teaspoon cayenne pepper
1 cup olive oil or vegetable oil
$\frac{2}{3}$ cup lemon juice

- Cook the pasta using the package directions; drain. Rinse with cold water; drain. Place in a large salad bowl. Add the garbanzo beans, pepperoni, olives, bell peppers, mushrooms, garlic, basil, oregano, salt, black pepper and cayenne pepper and mix well.
- Combine the olive oil and lemon juice in a jar with a tight-fitting lid. Cover the jar and shake. Pour over the salad and toss. Chill, covered, for 6 hours or longer. Stir before serving.
- *Yield: 12 to 16 servings*

Chicken Mexicali Salad

2 cups shredded lettuce
1 (15-ounce) can kidney beans,
  drained
2 medium tomatoes, chopped
1 to 2 tablespoons chopped
  green chiles

$\frac{1}{2}$ cup chopped black olives
4 sliced grilled chicken breasts
Mexicali Dressing
Picante sauce to taste
1 cup shredded Cheddar cheese
$\frac{1}{2}$ cup crushed corn chips

- Combine the lettuce, beans, tomatoes, green chiles and olives in a large bowl and toss to combine. Layer the lettuce mixture, chicken, Mexicali Dressing, picante sauce, half the cheese, the corn chips and the remaining cheese in a large bowl.
- *Yield: 8 to 10 servings*

Mexicali Dressing

1 large avocado, mashed
$\frac{1}{2}$ cup sour cream
2 tablespoons Italian dressing

1 teaspoon minced onion
$\frac{3}{4}$ teaspoon chili powder
$\frac{1}{4}$ teaspoon salt

- Combine the avocado, sour cream, Italian dressing, onion, chili powder and salt in a bowl and mix well.

MUCHO MEXICANA

This festive menu is best served on the patio with lots of candles in small clay pots. Remember all those odd colored cloth napkins you own? Well, mix the colors and create your own fiesta on your patio table. The lasagna can be made well ahead, which always helps the host or hostess. Chill some Mexican beer and whip up a pitcher of margaritas for refreshments.

South of the Border Lasagna
Chicken Mexicali Salad
Oven-Roasted Vegetables
Orzo Medley
Black Bean and Corn Salsa
Mexican Corn Muffins
Mint Dazzler

Fettuccini and Chicken Niçoise Salad

1 pound poached chicken breast,
   shredded or sliced into
   thin strips
3 medium tomatoes, chopped
¼ cup capers, rinsed, drained
¾ cup mayonnaise

2 tablespoons chopped fresh dill
1 teaspoon salt
1 teaspoon freshly ground
   pepper
12 ounces fettuccini

- Combine the chicken, tomatoes, capers, mayonnaise, dill, salt and pepper in a large bowl and mix well. Chill, covered, for 4 hours or longer.
- Cook the pasta using the package directions until al dente; drain. Rinse with cold water; drain. Add to the chicken mixture and mix well. Chill, covered, in the refrigerator.
- *Yield: 6 servings*

Curried Shrimp Salad

2 cups cooked rice
1 (10-ounce) package frozen
   green peas, thawed
½ cup chopped celery
½ cup sliced green onions

1 tablespoon curry powder
1 tablespoon lemon juice
2 pounds cooked peeled shrimp
1 cup mayonnaise

- Combine the rice, peas, celery, green onions, curry powder, lemon juice, shrimp and mayonnaise in a bowl and mix well. Chill, covered, for 24 hours or longer.
- *Yield: 4 to 6 servings*

Rémoulade Pasta

8 ounces large shell macaroni

2 cups mayonnaise

½ cup Dijon mustard

¼ cup ketchup

4 teaspoons horseradish

2 teaspoons Worcestershire sauce

3 tablespoons lemon juice

1 teaspoon Tabasco sauce (optional)

2 pounds boiled shrimp, peeled, deveined

¾ cup chopped parsley

½ cup finely chopped onion

¼ cup capers, drained

- Cook the pasta using the package directions; drain.
- Combine the mayonnaise, mustard, ketchup, horseradish, Worcestershire sauce, lemon juice and Tabasco sauce in a blender container and process until smooth.
- Combine the cooked pasta, shrimp, parsley, onion and capers in a bowl. Add half the mayonnaise mixture and mix well. Add additional mayonnaise mixture to make of the desired consistency. Reserve the remaining mayonnaise mixture for another use.
- *Yield: 4 to 6 servings*

GARLIC-INFUSED OIL

1 garlic bulb (at least 10 cloves)
2 cups oil (not olive oil)

Crush the garlic with a garlic press into a pint jar. Fill with oil, cover tightly and refrigerate. Use only the oil for a mild garlic flavor. Add pieces of garlic for a stronger flavor. Uses include salad dressings, sauces, pasta and basting for meats and seafood.

Hot Fruit Compote

1 (15-ounce) can pears
1 (15-ounce) can peaches
1 (20-ounce) can pineapple
   chunks
1 (17-ounce) can apricot
   halves
1/2 cup (1 stick) butter or
   margarine

1/2 cup cooking sherry
1/2 cup sugar
2 tablespoons flour
1 (14-ounce) jar spiced
   apple rings

- Drain the pears, peaches, pineapple chunks and apricot halves, reserving the juices. Arrange the fruit over the bottom of a large flat baking dish. Melt the butter in a saucepan over low heat. Add the sherry, sugar and 1/2 cup of the reserved fruit juices. Dissolve the flour in a small amount of cold water in a cup. Stir into the juice mixture. Cook until thickened, stirring constantly. Pour over the fruit. Chill, covered, for 8 to 12 hours.
- Drain the apple rings. Arrange over the top of the compote. Bake at 350 degrees for 45 minutes.
- *Yield: 6 to 8 servings*

"Good" Salad Dressing

8 teaspoons heavy cream
4 teaspoons minced garlic
1/4 cup salt
2 tablespoons pepper
1/4 cup dry mustard

2 3/4 cups sugar
1 1/2 cups apple cider vinegar
1 1/2 cups balsamic vinegar
3 cups olive oil
3 cups vegetable oil

- Combine the cream and garlic in a bowl. Chill, covered, for 8 to 12 hours. Combine the salt, pepper, mustard, sugar, cider vinegar, balsamic vinegar, olive oil and vegetable oil in a large bowl and mix well. Stir in the cream mixture. Store, covered, in the refrigerator.
- *Yield: about 9 cups*

Side Dishes

Bosc Pears
Wanda Stepp

Wanda Stepp

Wanda Stepp's Bosc Pears, *painted in oil, is one of her paintings from the Time and Tide series. She chooses objects for their symbolic values — drawn to objects past their prime — worn creased linens, overripe fruit, dead flowers, disfigured trees, etc. — not in a morbid sense but as beautiful, elegant survivors of the passage of time and tide.*

Wanda Stepp, a Rock Hill resident, has been a working artist for over fifteen years. She has won awards from the South Carolina State Fair, Invitational Art Exhibition at the University of South Carolina, and the Jubilee Juried Show. Her work can be seen in private and public collections throughout the Southeast.

Mrs. Ratterree's Asparagus Casserole

Mrs. Hiram Hutchison (Linda Dunbar), Past President, 1976–1977

1 (15-ounce) can cut asparagus
   spears, drained
1¼ cups crushed saltines
1 cup milk
1 cup shredded sharp cheese
1 (2-ounce) jar pimentos,
   chopped

3 eggs, beaten
1 teaspoon salt
⅛ teaspoon pepper
½ cup (1 stick) margarine,
   melted

- Combine the asparagus, saltines, milk, cheese, pimentos, eggs, salt and pepper in a bowl and mix well. Spoon into a greased 8×8-inch baking dish. Pour the margarine over the top.
- Bake at 350 degrees for 30 minutes or until set and brown around the edge.
- *Yield: 4 to 6 servings*

Oven-Roasted Asparagus

1 pound asparagus
2 garlic cloves, slivered
2 tablespoons water
2 tablespoons dry white wine or
   nonalcoholic white wine

2 teaspoons lemon juice
1 teaspoon olive oil
¼ teaspoon salt
⅛ teaspoon pepper

- Trim any tough ends from the asparagus spears and discard. Remove the peel from the bottom halves of the asparagus.
- Sprinkle the garlic over the bottom of a 9×13-inch baking dish. Arrange the asparagus in a single layer over the garlic. Combine the water, wine, lemon juice, olive oil, salt and pepper in a bowl and mix well. Pour over the asparagus.
- Bake at 400 degrees for 10 minutes. Turn the asparagus over. Roast for an additional 8 to 10 minutes or until the asparagus is tender-crisp and the liquid is almost evaporated.
- *Yield: 4 servings*

SIDE DISHES

PAST PRESIDENTS

This asparagus casserole recipe was given to my mother, Louise Dunbar, in the mid-1940s. She named the casserole after Mrs. A. E. Ratterree, who shared it with her. Both ladies were wonderful cooks. It became a family holiday tradition to have this casserole for dinner, and I have kept this tradition in our home.

When I had the Annual Board Luncheon at my home in 1977, my mother helped prepare the lunch. Of course we had this casserole, and it was a huge success.

—Mrs. Hiram Hutchison (Linda Dunbar)

New Orleans Red Beans and Rice

A NIGHT IN OLD NEW ORLEANS

Dixieland jazz will set the mood for this night in the "Big Easy." Red beans and rice are traditionally served on Mondays by cooks in New Orleans, but your guests will enjoy them anytime. Is it hot and humid in here, or is it just me?

New Orleans Red Beans and Rice
Seafood Jambalaya
Creole-Style Tomatoes and Corn
Okra and Tomatoes
Fresh French Bread
Bourbon Cake with Praline Ice Cream

1 pound dried red kidney beans
2 bay leaves
1 large onion, chopped
3 ribs celery, chopped
1/2 large green bell pepper, chopped
Butter for sautéing
3 garlic cloves, minced
1 teaspoon crushed thyme
8 ounces ham, cut into 1-inch pieces
1 (1-pound) package smoked sausage or light sausage
Hot cooked rice

- Sort and rinse the beans; drain. Place the beans and bay leaves in a Dutch oven. Add water to a depth of 3 inches. Cook over medium heat.
- Sauté the onion, celery and bell pepper in a small amount of butter in a skillet until tender. Add the garlic. Sauté for 2 minutes. Add to the bean mixture with the thyme. Sauté the ham in the skillet until brown. Add to the bean mixture. Sauté the sausage in the skillet. Add to the bean mixture.
- Bring the bean mixture to a boil. Reduce the heat. Simmer, covered, for 2 hours or until the beans are tender. Remove the bay leaves. Mash a small amount of the beans in the pot and stir to combine. Adjust the seasonings. Serve over hot cooked rice.
- *Yield: 6 to 8 servings*

Grilled Corn with Cumin Scallion Butter

1 tablespoon cumin seeds
$^1/_2$ teaspoon kosher salt
$^3/_4$ cup (1$^1/_2$ sticks) unsalted butter
$^1/_3$ cup finely chopped scallions
1 teaspoon fresh lemon juice
12 ears of corn in husks

- Toast the cumin seeds in a small heavy skillet over medium heat for 1 minute or until fragrant, shaking the skillet constantly. Let stand until cool. Grind the toasted seeds and salt in a spice or coffee grinder.
- Combine the butter and cumin mixture in a saucepan. Heat until the butter is melted, stirring constantly. Stir in the scallions and lemon juice.
- Peel the husks from the corn, leaving the husks attached at the base of the ears. Remove the corn silk. Brush the kernels with the cumin scallion butter. Cover and chill the remaining butter in the refrigerator. Reassemble the husks over the ears. Peel off a few layers of husks and tear lengthwise into narrow strips. Tie the ends of the reassembled ears with strips of husk. You may prepare up to this point 1 day ahead and chill, covered, until ready to use.
- Grill the corn 5 to 6 inches from hot coals for 20 minutes, turning occasionally. You may bake in a shallow baking pan on the middle oven rack at 450 degrees for 35 minutes, turning occasionally.
- Reheat the remaining cumin scallion butter. Serve with the corn.
- *Yield: 8 servings*

Sweet Corn Pie

3 eggs
1 (16-ounce) can whole
   kernel corn, drained, or
   cream-style corn

$1/4$ cup ($1/2$ stick) butter, melted
$1/2$ cup sugar
$1^1/2$ cups evaporated milk

- Beat the eggs in a mixing bowl. Add the corn, butter, sugar and evaporated milk and mix well. Spoon into a pie plate. Bake at 300 degrees for 30 minutes or until set.
- *Yield: 4 servings*

Eggplant Zucchini Cheese Bake

1 large eggplant, peeled, cubed
2 tablespoons butter
2 medium zucchini, sliced
1 medium onion, chopped

1 to 2 cups shredded cheese
1 large tomato, sliced
1 teaspoon salt
$1/2$ teaspoon pepper

- Bring enough water to cover the eggplant to a boil in a saucepan. Add the eggplant. Cook until tender; drain.
- Heat the butter in a skillet until melted. Add the zucchini and onion. Sauté until tender-crisp. Remove from the heat. Add the eggplant and mix well.
- Layer half the zucchini mixture, half the cheese, the remaining zucchini mixture and tomato slices in a baking dish. Sprinkle with the salt and pepper. Sprinkle the remaining cheese over the top. Bake at 350 degrees for 30 minutes.
- *Yield: 6 to 8 servings*

Green Beans in Sour Cream

**2 pounds fresh green beans, cut into 1¹/₂-inch pieces, or
   2 (16-ounce) cans French-cut green beans**

Salt to taste

1 medium onion, thinly sliced

**2 tablespoons finely chopped fresh parsley, or 2 teaspoons
   dried parsley**

2 tablespoons butter or margarine, melted

2 tablespoons flour

1 teaspoon salt

¹/₄ teaspoon pepper

1 cup sour cream

1 cup buttered bread crumbs

- Bring enough water to cover the fresh green beans and a small amount
  of salt to a boil in a saucepan. Add the green beans. Cook for 20 minutes
  or until tender-crisp; drain.
- Sauté the onion and parsley in the butter in a skillet until tender. Reduce
  the heat. Stir in the flour, 1 teaspoon salt and pepper. Cook until bubbly,
  stirring constantly. Add the sour cream. Cook until heated through,
  stirring constantly. Stir in the beans. Spoon into a greased 2-quart
  casserole. Sprinkle the bread crumbs over the top. Bake at 350 degrees for
  20 minutes.
- You may substitute crisp-fried crumbled bacon for the bread crumbs and
  bacon drippings for the butter.
- *Yield: 8 servings*

SIDE DISHES

BLANCHING VEGETABLES

*Want to keep your vegetables
firm for a pretty presentation?
It's easy. Put your cleaned
vegetables, such as broccoli,
in a wire mesh basket and
lower into boiling water.
Boil for a few minutes until
desired tenderness. Pull the
basket out of the boiling
water and immediately
plunge into a large bowl of ice
water to cover. Your vegetables
will retain their bright color
and won't fall apart!*

Green Beans with Tomatoes and Feta

2 (16-ounce) packages frozen French-cut green beans, thawed	2 tablespoons fresh lemon juice
	1/4 teaspoon salt
1 teaspoon olive oil	1/2 teaspoon freshly ground pepper
2 garlic cloves, minced	
2 teaspoons Italian seasoning	1 (4-ounce) package crumbled feta cheese
4 plum tomatoes, chopped	1/4 cup pine nuts, toasted

• Drain the green beans, pressing out the excess moisture. Heat the oil in a large nonstick skillet until hot. Add the garlic and Italian seasoning. Cook over medium heat for 1 minute. Add the green beans. Cook for 5 to 7 minutes. Stir in the tomatoes. Cook for 2 minutes or until heated through, stirring constantly. Stir in the lemon juice, salt and pepper. Sprinkle with the feta cheese and pine nuts.

• *Yield: 6 servings*

Okra and Tomatoes

2 tablespoons bacon drippings	2 garlic cloves, minced
1 pound okra, sliced	1 bay leaf
1 medium onion, chopped	1/2 teaspoon thyme, crushed
1 (16-ounce) can tomatoes	Salt and pepper to taste

• Heat the bacon drippings in a large skillet over medium heat until melted. Add the okra and onion. Sauté for 20 minutes, stirring constantly.

• Add the undrained tomatoes, garlic, bay leaf, thyme, salt and pepper. Reduce the heat. Simmer, covered, for 30 minutes. Remove the bay leaf.

• *Yield: 4 or 5 servings*

Grilled Onion Slices

1/2 cup (1 stick) butter or
  margarine, melted
3 tablespoons Dijon
  mustard
2 teaspoons wine vinegar

1 tablespoon chopped fresh
  parsley or tarragon
3 large red onions, cut crosswise
  into 1/2-inch slices
Salt and pepper to taste

- Combine the butter, mustard, vinegar and parsley in a bowl and mix well. Add the onions, stirring to coat. Drain, reserving the marinade.
- Place the onions on a grill over hot coals. Sprinkle with salt and pepper. Grill for 10 minutes or until tender and golden brown, turning and basting 2 or 3 times with the reserved marinade.
- *Yield: 6 servings*

Gourmet Potatoes

5 pounds potatoes
2 medium onions, chopped
1 pound mushrooms, sliced
3/4 cup (1 1/2 sticks) butter
1 cup hot milk

1/4 cup (1/2 stick) butter, melted
Salt and pepper to taste
1 cup sour cream
Paprika to taste

- Peel the potatoes and cut into large pieces. Combine with enough water to cover in a saucepan. Bring to a boil. Boil until tender; drain.
- Sauté the onions and mushrooms in 3/4 cup butter in a skillet for 2 minutes. Remove the onions and mushrooms, reserving the butter.
- Beat the potatoes in a mixing bowl until smooth. Add the hot milk, reserved butter, 1/4 cup melted butter, salt and pepper.
- Spread one-third of the potatoes over the bottom of a greased 9×13-inch baking dish. Layer the onion mixture, sour cream and remaining potatoes one-half at a time over the potato layer. Sprinkle with paprika. Bake at 350 degrees for 30 minutes.
- *Yield: 8 to 10 servings*

Spinach and Artichoke Casserole

½ cup mayonnaise	¼ cup chopped onion
¼ cup sour cream	¼ cup chopped celery (optional)
2 (10-ounce) packages frozen spinach, cooked, drained	1 tablespoon Parmesan cheese
1 (14-ounce) can artichokes, drained	¼ cup shredded Swiss cheese
	Dash of lemon juice
1 (8-ounce) can sliced water chestnuts, drained	Garlic salt to taste
	Salt and pepper to taste
	Bread crumbs

- Combine the mayonnaise and sour cream in a large bowl and mix well. Add the spinach, artichokes, water chestnuts, onion, celery, Parmesan cheese, Swiss cheese, lemon juice, garlic salt, salt and pepper and mix well. Spoon into a baking dish. Sprinkle bread crumbs over the top. Bake at 350 degrees for 20 minutes.
- *Yield: 8 servings*

Posh Squash

2 pounds yellow squash	1 cup mayonnaise
¼ cup chopped green bell pepper	1 cup shredded sharp cheese
1 medium onion, chopped	Salt and pepper to taste
2 eggs	Bread crumbs

- Bring enough water to cover the vegetables to a boil in a saucepan. Add the squash, bell pepper and onion. Cook until tender-crisp; drain.
- Beat the eggs in a large mixing bowl. Add the mayonnaise, cheese, salt and pepper and mix well. Stir in the cooked squash mixture. Spoon into a buttered baking dish. Bake at 350 degrees for 25 minutes. Sprinkle bread crumbs over the top. Bake for an additional 5 minutes.
- *Yield: 6 to 8 servings*

Squash Casserole

½ cup (1 stick) butter

4 cups thinly sliced yellow squash

1 cup chopped onion

2 teaspoons parsley

½ teaspoon basil

½ teaspoon pepper

½ teaspoon minced garlic

½ teaspoon salt

¼ teaspoon oregano

2 eggs

8 ounces mozzarella cheese, shredded

1 (8-count) can crescent rolls

2 teaspoons mustard

- Heat the butter in a skillet until melted. Add the squash and onion. Cook until tender. Stir in the parsley, basil, pepper, garlic powder, salt and oregano. Remove from the heat.
- Combine the eggs and cheese in a large bowl and mix well. Add the squash mixture and mix well.
- Unroll the crescent rolls. Arrange over the bottom of a 7×11-inch baking dish, pressing the perforations to seal. Spread the mustard over the dough. Spoon the squash mixture over the dough.
- Bake at 375 degrees for 18 to 20 minutes. Let stand for 10 minutes.
- *Yield: 8 to 10 servings*

SIDE DISHES

POEM

May the warp be the white light of morning,
May the weft be the red light of evening,
May the fringes be the falling rain,
May the border be the standing snow,
Thus weave for us a garment of brightness.

—Attributed to a North American Indian

Candied Sweet Potatoes

Mrs. James Perry (Angie), President, 2000–2001

4 or 5 medium sweet potatoes, cooked, peeled
1/2 cup chopped pecans
2 cups sugar
1 tablespoon cornstarch
1/2 teaspoon nutmeg
1/2 teaspoon cinnamon
1 cup water
2 tablespoons lemon juice
2 tablespoons butter
1 cup miniature marshmallows

- Cut the sweet potatoes into 3/8-inch slices. Arrange the slices in a buttered 9×13-inch baking dish. Sprinkle the pecans over the sweet potatoes.
- Combine the sugar, cornstarch, nutmeg and cinnamon in a saucepan and mix well. Add the water, lemon juice and butter. Bring to a boil, stirring occasionally. Boil for 1 minute. Pour over the sweet potatoes.
- Bake at 350 degrees for 40 minutes, basting 2 or 3 times with the syrup. Sprinkle the marshmallows over the top. Bake for an additional 5 minutes.
- *Yield: 6 servings*

Herb Tomatoes

2 (16-ounce) cans tomatoes
2 cups 1/2-inch cubes bread
1/2 cup (1 stick) margarine, melted
1/2 teaspoon salt
2 tablespoons sugar or artificial sweetener
1 teaspoon each oregano, parsley and crumbled rosemary

- Drain the tomatoes, reserving 1/4 cup of the juice. Cut the tomatoes into halves if small and quarters if large. Arrange in a single layer over the bottom of a greased 6×10-inch baking dish. Combine the bread cubes and margarine in a bowl and mix well. Arrange between the tomatoes. Pour the reserved tomato juice over the top. Sprinkle with the salt, sugar, oregano, parsley and rosemary. Bake at 350 degrees for 20 minutes.
- *Yield: 6 to 8 servings*

Creole-Style Tomatoes and Corn

2 slices bacon, chopped
1 large onion, chopped
1 medium green bell pepper, chopped
2 cups corn kernels
2¹/₂ cups chopped peeled tomatoes
¹/₂ bay leaf
¹/₄ teaspoon salt
¹/₈ teaspoon pepper

- Cook the bacon in a large skillet until crisp. Remove the bacon, reserving the drippings. Crumble the bacon and set aside.
- Sauté the onion and bell pepper in the reserved bacon drippings until tender. Add the corn, tomatoes and bay leaf. Bring to a boil. Reduce the heat. Simmer for 5 minutes, stirring occasionally. Stir in the salt and pepper. Remove the bay leaf. Sprinkle the bacon over the top.
- *Yield: 6 servings*

Oven-Roasted Vegetables

4 small zucchini, cut into 1-inch slices
4 small yellow squash, cut into 1-inch slices
2 large purple onions, cut into 1-inch slices
2 teaspoons olive oil
2 teaspoons oregano
¹/₂ teaspoon salt
¹/₂ teaspoon pepper
2 large red bell peppers, cut into strips
2 large yellow bell peppers, cut into strips
2 teaspoons balsamic vinegar
¹/₄ cup chopped fresh parsley

- Arrange the zucchini, yellow squash and onions over the bottom of a greased large roasting pan. Drizzle the olive oil over the zucchini mixture. Sprinkle with the oregano, salt and pepper. Bake at 500 degrees for 10 minutes. Add the bell peppers to the zucchini mixture and toss gently. Bake for an additional 10 minutes. Drizzle with the balsamic vinegar. Sprinkle with the parsley. Toss to combine.
- *Yield: 8 to 10 servings*

Savannah Red Rice

½ cup (1 stick) butter

1 cup chopped green bell pepper

1 cup chopped celery

1 cup chopped Vidalia onion

3 cups long grain white rice

Olive oil

3 cups tomato sauce

1 (8-ounce) can tomato paste

Salt to taste

Pinch of sugar

- Heat the butter in a skillet until melted. Add the bell pepper, celery and onion. Sauté until tender-crisp.
- Place the rice in a large saucepan. Stir in enough olive oil to coat the rice. Add the tomato sauce and tomato paste and mix well. Cook, covered, until the rice is fluffy, stirring with a fork as needed to separate the grains. Stir in the bell pepper mixture. Cook until the rice is tender. Stir in the salt and sugar.
- You may top this with crisp-fried crumbled bacon or boiled shrimp.
- *Yield: 10 to 12 servings*

Cranberry Wild Rice

2 tablespoons butter

1 cup chopped onion

1 (16-ounce) can whole cranberry sauce

2 (6-ounce) packages Uncle Ben's long grain and wild rice

1½ cups thinly sliced celery

- Heat the butter in a 10-inch skillet until melted. Add the onion. Cook until tender. Add enough water to the cranberry sauce to measure 4½ cups. Add to the onion. Add the rice and seasoning packets to the cranberry mixture and mix well. Bring to a boil. Cook, tightly covered, over low heat for 25 minutes or until the liquid is absorbed. Stir in the celery.
- *Yield: 8 servings*

Wild Rice, Mushrooms and Asparagus

Mrs. C. Y. Workman, Jr. (Frances Stone), Past President, 1969–1970

1 (6-ounce) package Uncle Ben's long grain and wild rice
¹/₂ cup chopped pecans or almonds
1 (3-ounce) can sliced mushrooms
1 tablespoon butter
1 tablespoon flour
¹/₄ teaspoon salt
Dash of pepper
³/₄ cup milk
3 ounces cream cheese, softened
1 pound asparagus, trimmed

- Prepare the rice using the package directions. Stir in the pecans. Drain the mushrooms, reserving the liquid.
- Heat the butter in a skillet until melted. Stir in the flour, salt and pepper. Cook until bubbly. Remove from the heat. Add the reserved mushroom juice and milk, whisking constantly. Cook until thickened, stirring constantly. Add the cream cheese, whisking until smooth. Stir in the mushrooms.
- Bring enough water to cover the asparagus to a boil in a saucepan. Add the asparagus. Cook until tender-crisp; drain.
- Spoon the rice onto a serving plate. Arrange the asparagus over the rice. Spoon the mushroom sauce over the asparagus.
- *Yield: 4 to 6 servings*

My mother, Zula Driggers White from Hartsville, gave this dressing recipe to me. Chick's family, all thirty-four of them, have gathered at our house every Thanksgiving for many years. Many of them have said that it wouldn't be Thanksgiving without Aunt Linda's dressing.

—Mrs. Charles C. Williams
(Linda Driggers)

Orzo Medley

¹/₂ cup orzo, cooked

1 or 2 (15-ounce) cans black beans, rinsed, drained

1 (15-ounce) can whole kernel corn, drained

¹/₂ cup chopped red onion

¹/₂ cup chopped red bell pepper

¹/₄ cup chopped fresh cilantro

¹/₄ cup cider vinegar

1¹/₂ teaspoons Dijon mustard

³/₄ teaspoon cumin

¹/₂ teaspoon minced garlic

¹/₂ cup olive oil

¹/₄ teaspoon salt

¹/₂ teaspoon pepper

- Combine the orzo, black beans, corn, onion, bell pepper and cilantro in a sealable container and mix well. Combine the remaining ingredients in a bowl and mix well. Pour over the orzo mixture. Seal the container.
- Marinate in the refrigerator for 8 hours or longer.
- *Yield: 8 to 10 servings*

Thanksgiving Dressing

Mrs. Charles C. Williams (Linda Driggers), Past President, 1982–1983

1 large onion, finely chopped

¹/₂ cup finely chopped celery

¹/₂ cup (1 stick) butter

8 cups crumbled corn bread

4 cups toasted white bread crumbs

1 tablespoon poultry seasoning

1 tablespoon crumbled dry sage

Salt and pepper to taste

3 cups (or more) turkey broth or pan drippings

- Cook the onion and celery in the butter in a skillet until tender. Combine the onion mixture, corn bread, white bread crumbs, poultry seasoning, sage, salt and pepper in a large bowl and mix well. Stir in enough broth to make a very moist mixture. Spoon into a greased baking dish.
- Bake at 375 degrees for 45 minutes or until golden brown.
- *Yield: 12 servings*

Cranberry Relish

1 pound fresh cranberries

2 oranges, separated into
    sections

2 unpeeled medium red tart
    apples, cut into pieces

2 cups sugar

1 (15-ounce) can crushed
    pineapple, drained

1/2 cup pecans

1 cup chopped celery

- Grind the cranberries, oranges and apples. Place in a bowl. Add the sugar, pineapple, pecans and celery and mix well. Chill, covered, for 3 days or longer.
- *Yield: 8 to 10 servings*

Cranberry Apple Casserole

3 cups chopped unpeeled apples

2 cups fresh cranberries

1 1/4 cups sugar

1/2 cup packed brown sugar

1/3 cup flour

1 1/2 cups rolled oats

1/3 cup (or more) nuts

1/2 cup (1 stick) margarine,
    melted

- Combine the apples, cranberries, sugar, brown sugar and flour in a baking dish and mix well. Spread evenly over the bottom of the dish. Combine the oats, nuts and margarine in a bowl and mix well. Sprinkle over the cranberry mixture.
- Bake at 350 degrees for 1 hour. You may freeze the casserole before baking.
- *Yield: 10 to 12 servings*

Black Bean and Corn Salsa

1 (15-ounce) can black beans, drained
1 (15-ounce) can white Shoe Peg corn, drained
1 green bell pepper, chopped
1 red bell pepper, chopped

1 red onion, chopped
1 (4-ounce) package crumbled feta cheese
1 cup Italian dressing
Tortilla chips

- Combine the beans, corn, bell peppers, onion, feta cheese and dressing in a bowl and mix well. Chill, covered, for 2 hours or longer. Serve with tortilla chips.
- *Yield: 8 servings*

Okra Pickles

3^1/$_2$ pounds small whole okra pods
8 teaspoons sugar
8 small hot peppers, cut into halves

4 teaspoons dillseeds
4^1/$_2$ cups water
4^1/$_2$ cups cider vinegar
^{1}/$_2$ cup salt

- Pack the okra into 8 hot sterilized 1-pint jars. Place 1 teaspoon sugar, 2 pepper halves and ^{1}/$_2$ teaspoon dillseeds in each jar.
- Combine the water, cider vinegar and salt in a saucepan. Bring to a boil. Pour the boiling syrup into the jars, leaving ^{1}/$_4$ inch headspace; seal with 2-piece lids. Process in a boiling water bath for 15 minutes.
- *Yield: 8 pints pickles*

Frozen Morning Awakening
Kathy Caudill

Meats

Kathy Caudill

Kathy Caudill's Frozen Morning Awakening *illustrates her ability to capture the emotion or feeling of ordinary people, places, and things that are familiar and that have special meaning. She creates an almost magical aura of the first beams of sunlight streaking through the barn above the cattle huddled together for warmth.*

Kathy Caudill, a third generation artist and a Rock Hill resident, has been painting full-time for more than twenty years. Kathy has won more than two hundred awards, including top awards from the South Carolina and West Virginia Watercolor Societies. She is the author of Landscapes in Watercolor *and has exhibited in such shows as "North America Day Invitational" in Tielt, Belgium, and "April in Appalachia" in Blacksburg, Virginia. Her work can be seen in both national and international collections.*

Beef Brisket

2 onions, coarsely chopped
1 (4-pound) beef brisket
2 garlic cloves, crushed
Pepper to taste
1 tablespoon Worcestershire sauce
2 envelopes onion soup mix
1 (12-ounce) bottle chili sauce
1 (12-ounce) can beer
3 slices rye bread

- Arrange the onions over the bottom of a roasting pan. Rub the brisket with the garlic. Place over the onions. Sprinkle the pepper over the brisket. Drizzle the Worcestershire sauce over the brisket. Sprinkle the onion soup mixes over the brisket. Pour the chili sauce and the beer over the brisket. Tear the bread into small pieces. Tuck under the brisket so that the liquid is covering the bread.
- Bake, tightly covered, at 350 degrees for 45 minutes. Reduce the temperature to 275 degrees. Cook for an additional 2 1/4 hours, checking occasionally to ensure that the liquid covers the bread. Remove to a serving platter.
- Combine the bread, half of the onions and 2 cups of the liquid from the roasting pan in a blender container. Process until smooth. Pour into the pan and mix well. Serve with the brisket.
- *Yield: 10 to 12 servings*

London Broil

As I reflect, I remember cooking in my Aunt Sadie's kitchen. My children now enjoy this same experience.

—Mrs. Kyle E. Melton (Robin Allen)

Mrs. Kyle E. Melton (Robin Allen), Past President, 1997–1998

**1 (4- to 5-pound) London broil or sirloin steak,
    at room temperature**
Vegetable oil for browning
1½ teaspoons salt
½ teaspoon freshly ground pepper
1¼ teaspoons rosemary
½ cup red wine
1 tablespoon butter

- Brown the beef in hot oil in a skillet for 3 to 5 minutes on each side. Place the beef on a rack in a shallow roasting pan. Sprinkle with the salt, pepper and rosemary. Bake at 350 degrees for 25 to 30 minutes. Remove to a hot serving platter. Slice thinly cross grain.
- Add the wine to the roasting pan. Add the butter, stirring until butter is melted. Serve with the beef.
- *Yield: 8 servings*

Cajun Blackened Filet Mignon

1 (1½-pound) beef tenderloin
2 tablespoons Cajun blackened seasoning
¼ cup prepared horseradish
½ cup sour cream
Chopped green onions to taste

- Spray all sides of the beef with vegetable cooking spray. Sprinkle with the seasoning. Spray again with vegetable cooking spray. Heat a heavy ovenproof skillet over medium-high heat for 3 to 5 minutes. Add the beef. Cook for 3 to 4 minutes on each side.
- Bake at 400 degrees for 15 minutes or to 145 degrees, medium-rare, on a meat thermometer. Let stand for 10 minutes. Cut into 24 slices. Arrange on a serving platter. Set aside, covering with foil to keep warm. Combine the horseradish and sour cream in a bowl and mix well. Place the green onions on a small plate. Serve the beef with the sour cream mixture and the green onions.
- *Yield: 12 servings*

Beef Tenderloin Steaks with Balsamic Sauce

4 (6-ounce) beef tenderloin
  steaks
2 tablespoons coarse-grain
  sea salt or regular salt
1 tablespoon coarsely ground
  pepper

2 tablespoons olive oil
Fresh thyme sprigs for garnish
Balsamic Sauce

- Rub the steaks with the salt and pepper. Brown the steaks over high heat in the hot olive oil in an ovenproof skillet for 2 to 3 minutes on each side.
- Bake at 350 degrees for 8 to 15 minutes or to desired degree of doneness. Remove to a serving plate. Garnish with fresh thyme sprigs. Serve immediately with Balsamic Sauce.
- *Yield: 4 servings*

Balsamic Sauce

¼ cup dry red wine
¼ cup dry sherry
3 tablespoons balsamic vinegar
1 shallot, chopped

2 garlic cloves, chopped
2 egg yolks, beaten
⅓ cup unsalted butter, melted

- Combine the wine, sherry, balsamic vinegar, shallot and garlic in a saucepan. Bring to a boil. Cook for 2 minutes. Remove from the heat. Stir a small amount of the hot mixture into the beaten egg yolks. Stir the egg yolks into the hot mixture. Cook over low heat until thickened, stirring constantly. Whisk in the butter gradually.

Steak au Poivre Vert

4 (½-inch-thick) steaks
¼ cup vegetable oil
Pinch of salt
¼ cup (½ stick) butter
3 tablespoons brandy
½ cup dry sherry or madeira
1 medium onion, chopped
2 tablespoons green peppercorns
2 tablespoons soy sauce
1 teaspoon vinegar
⅔ cup light cream
Pinch of paprika
1 tablespoon chopped fresh parsley

- Trim the steaks of any excess fat. Brush with a small amount of the oil. Season lightly with the salt.
- Heat the remaining oil and the butter in a skillet until hot. Brown the steaks for about 2 minutes on each side. Pour in the brandy. Ignite it and immediately add the sherry to quench the flames. Remove the steaks and keep warm.
- Add the onion, peppercorns, soy sauce and vinegar to the brandy mixture. Bring to a boil. Boil for 4 minutes. Stir in the cream and paprika. Boil for 1 minute.
- Place the steaks in the cream mixture. Cook for 1 minute on each side or until heated through. Remove to a serving plate. Pour the sauce over the steaks. Garnish with the parsley.
- *Yield: 4 servings*

Grillades

1 pound beef round steak,
   pounded thin
¼ cup vegetable oil
3 tablespoons flour
1 large onion, chopped
1 bell pepper, chopped
½ cup chopped celery
1 tablespoon chopped garlic
1 bay leaf
4 tomatoes, chopped, or
   1 (15-ounce) can tomatoes

Salt and black pepper to taste
Cayenne pepper to taste
Dash of Tabasco sauce
1 tablespoon parsley
2 cups water
1 beef bouillon cube
Cornstarch for thickening
   (optional)
Rice or grits

- Cut the steak into 2- to 3-inch round pieces. Brown the steak in a skillet. Remove and set aside. Add the oil and flour. Cook until brown, stirring constantly. Add the onion, bell pepper, celery and garlic. Sauté for 5 to 10 minutes or until vegetables are tender.
- Combine the steak, vegetable mixture, bay leaf, tomatoes, salt, black pepper, cayenne pepper, Tabasco sauce, parsley, water and bouillon cube in a large stockpot and mix well.
- Simmer, covered, for 45 minutes. Season to taste. Remove the bay leaf. You may thicken the sauce by mixing cornstarch with a small amount of hot water and stirring it into the grillades. Serve over rice or grits.
- *Yield: 4 to 6 servings*

Mongolian Beef

4 pounds sirloin steak
$1/4$ cup soy sauce
$1/4$ cup sherry
$1/4$ cup hoisin sauce
$1/4$ cup beef broth
2 tablespoons Worcestershire sauce
1 garlic clove, minced
$1/2$ teaspoon ground ginger
$1/4$ cup cornstarch
$1/4$ cup vegetable oil
4 carrots, shredded
3 onions, sliced
2 celery ribs, sliced diagonally
2 green bell peppers, cut into $1/4$-inch strips
4 cups shredded cabbage
1 (14-ounce) can bean sprouts

- Cut the steak into strips $1/4$ inch thick and 2 inches long. Combine the soy sauce and sherry in a sealable plastic bag. Add the steak. Marinate, in the refrigerator, for 30 minutes or longer. Drain, reserving the marinade.
- Combine the reserved marinade, hoisin sauce, beef broth, Worcestershire sauce, garlic, ginger and cornstarch in a bowl and mix well.
- Heat the oil in a wok. Stir-fry the beef for 2 minutes. Add the carrots, onions, celery, bell peppers, cabbage and bean sprouts and stir-fry. Stir in the marinade mixture. Bring to a boil. Boil for 2 to 3 minutes, stirring constantly. Cook until sauce is thickened, stirring frequently.
- *Yield: 8 to 12 servings*

HOW MUCH MEAT SHOULD YOU BUY?

Boneless Meats—about $1/4$ to $1/3$ pound per serving

Boneless Roasts—same as above

Small and medium bone in—about $1/2$ pound per serving

Large bone in—about $3/4$ pound per serving

Be sure to plan on more than one serving for hearty appetites.

Beef and Eggplant Stew

3 or 4 medium eggplant

Salt to taste

1 pound beef stew meat, cut into 1-inch cubes

2 tablespoons butter or margarine, or
   1¹/₂ tablespoons light vegetable oil

1 large onion, chopped

1 teaspoon turmeric

2¹/₂ cups water

1 teaspoon salt

¹/₂ teaspoon pepper

¹/₄ cup shortening or vegetable oil

4 large tomatoes, cut into halves

2 tablespoons tomato paste

¹/₄ cup warm water

White rice

- Peel and cut the eggplant lengthwise into ¹/₂-inch slices. Sprinkle both sides with salt to taste and place on paper towels.
- Brown the beef in the hot butter in a skillet. Add the onion. Cook until the onion is tender. Spoon into a 3-quart saucepan. Stir in the turmeric, 2¹/₂ cups water, 1 teaspoon salt and pepper. Bring to a boil. Reduce the heat to medium-low. Simmer for 30 minutes or until the beef is tender.
- Pat the eggplant slices firmly with paper towels to dry. Heat 1 tablespoon of the shortening in a skillet. Brown the eggplant on both sides in the hot shortening in batches, adding additional shortening if needed. Arrange on top of the beef mixture. Arrange the tomatoes, skin side up, over the eggplant.
- Dissolve the tomato paste in ¹/₄ cup warm water in a bowl. Pour over the tomatoes. Simmer, covered, over medium-low heat for 30 minutes. Serve over white rice.
- *Yield: 6 servings*

Beef and Vegetable Fried Rice

1 pound ground beef
2 garlic cloves, minced
1/4 teaspoon ground ginger
1 red bell pepper, sliced
1 (10-ounce) package frozen
  pea pods
2 teaspoons vegetable oil

3 cups cold cooked rice
2 teaspoons sesame oil
3 tablespoons soy sauce
1/4 cup chopped green onions
1 (8-ounce) can water chestnuts,
  drained

- Brown the ground beef with the garlic and ginger over medium heat in a skillet for 8 to 10 minutes, stirring until crumbly; drain. Remove the beef.
- Stir-fry the bell pepper and pea pods in the hot vegetable oil in a skillet. Add the rice, sesame oil, and soy sauce and mix well. Stir in the green onions and water chestnuts.
- Spoon the rice mixture into a serving bowl. Arrange the beef over the top.
- *Yield: 4 to 6 servings*

Beefy Creole Corn Casserole

6 slices bacon
1 pound ground beef
1 onion, chopped
1 (10-ounce) can tomato soup
1/2 cup cornmeal

2 eggs, lightly beaten
2 cups milk
1 (15-ounce) can whole
  kernel corn

- Cook the bacon in a skillet until crisp; drain. Crumble the bacon. Brown the ground beef with the onion in the skillet, stirring until crumbly; drain. Add the crumbled bacon, soup and cornmeal and mix well. Cook over low heat for 5 minutes. Add the eggs, milk and corn and mix well. Spoon into a greased 9×13-inch baking dish. Bake at 325 degrees for 1 hour.
- *Yield: 4 to 6 servings*

JAPANESE TEA BIRTHDAY PARTY FOR YOUNG GIRLS

Bathrobes become kimonos and chopsticks double as hair accessories for this precious birthday party. Honorable Father and Mother serve the girls tea and lunch at a low table with pillows to kneel on. (Use cinder blocks with a long piece of plywood covered with a tablecloth or a large coffee table.) The girls are sure to love the Beef and Vegetable Fried Rice as the main course. (It's Chinese in origin but children love it!) Crafts to make can include tissue paper Lotus flowers and maps of Japan to color. A smile is sure to grace every child's face until it is time to say "Sayonara."

MEATS

SWEETHEARTS SUPPER

Invite a few couples to share a romantic Italian dinner. Red plaid tablecloths, votive candles, chianti, and soft violin music will set the mood.

Raspberry Black Bean Dip

Brattonsville Cheese Mold

Lasagna with Béchamel Sauce

Mixed Green Salad with

   "Good" Salad Dressing

Dobash Torte with

   French Buttercream Frosting

White Wine Cake

Lasagna with Béchamel Sauce

2 pounds ground beef

8 ounces fresh sliced mushrooms

2 onions, chopped

1 celery rib, chopped

1/2 green bell pepper, chopped

3 tablespoons olive oil

4 tomatoes, peeled, chopped

1 tablespoon minced garlic

1/4 cup chopped fresh parsley

1 teaspoon basil

1 bay leaf

1 teaspoon each oregano, rosemary and thyme

Salt and pepper to taste

1 cup water

1 (16-ounce) package whole grain lasagna noodles, cooked

Béchamel Sauce

1 cup shredded mozzarella cheese

- Place the ground beef in a roasting pan. Brown under the broiler, stirring frequently; drain. Sauté the mushrooms, onions, celery and bell pepper in the hot olive oil in a skillet until the onions are translucent. Stir in the tomatoes. Add the next 7 ingredients and mix well. Bring to a boil. Add the water and ground beef. Bring to a boil. Reduce the heat. Simmer for 2 hours. Season with salt and pepper. Remove the bay leaf.
- Layer the noodles, meat sauce, Béchamel sauce and mozzarella cheese one-half at a time in a greased baking dish. Bake at 350 degrees for 30 to 45 minutes or until hot and bubbly.
- *Yield: 8 servings*

Béchamel Sauce

2 tablespoons butter

2 tablespoons stone ground whole wheat flour

1 cup milk

1 cup shredded mozzarella cheese

1/4 teaspoon nutmeg

Salt and pepper to taste

- Heat the butter in a skillet until melted. Add the flour. Cook for 2 minutes, stirring constantly. Add the milk, whisking constantly. Bring to a simmer. Simmer until thickened. Stir in the mozzarella cheese. Reduce the heat. Simmer for 2 additional minutes. Stir in the nutmeg, salt and pepper.

South of the Border Lasagna

2 pounds ground chuck
1 onion, chopped
1 garlic clove, minced
2 tablespoons chili powder
3 cups tomato sauce
1 teaspoon sugar
1 tablespoon salt
1/2 cup sliced black olives
1 (4-ounce) can chopped
    green chiles
Vegetable oil
12 corn tortillas
2 cups small curd cottage cheese

1 egg
8 ounces Monterey Jack cheese,
    shredded
1 cup shredded Cheddar cheese
1/2 cup chopped green onions
    (optional)
1/2 cup sour cream (optional)
1/2 cup sliced black olives
    (optional)
1 cup chopped pecans (optional)
1 cup raisins (optional)
1 cup sour cream (optional)

- Brown the ground chuck in a skillet, stirring until crumbly; drain. Add the onion and garlic. Cook until onion is tender. Sprinkle the chili powder over the beef mixture and mix well.
- Add the tomato sauce, sugar, salt, 1/2 cup olives and green chiles and mix well. Bring to a simmer. Simmer for 15 minutes, stirring occasionally.
- Heat oil in a skillet. Soften the tortillas in the hot oil. Drain on paper towels. Beat the cottage cheese and egg in a bowl.
- Spread one-third of the meat sauce over the bottom of a 9×13-inch baking dish. Layer the Monterey Jack cheese, cottage cheese mixture, tortillas and the remaining meat mixture half at a time. Sprinkle the Cheddar cheese over the layers.
- Bake at 350 degrees for 30 minutes. Combine the green onions, 1/2 cup sour cream and 1/2 cup olives in a bowl and mix well. Combine the pecans, raisins and 1 cup sour cream in a separate bowl and mix well. Serve the lasagna with the green onion mixture and the pecan mixture.
- *Yield: 8 to 10 servings*

These burgers are quick, easy and delicious! The Kelletts loved this recipe with French fries and lots of ketchup.

—Virginia Ann Jones Kellett

Mushroom Burgers

Virginia Ann Jones Kellett, Past President, 1962–1963

1 (3-ounce) can chopped mushrooms
1 pound ground beef
4 ounces sharp cheese, shredded
1/2 teaspoon salt
Dash of pepper
1 teaspoon Worcestershire sauce
6 hamburger buns
2 tablespoons butter or margarine
1 teaspoon Kitchen Bouquet
6 slices bacon

- Combine the mushrooms, ground beef, cheese, salt, pepper and Worcestershire sauce in a bowl and mix well. Shape into 6 patties.
- Split the buns. Place a patty on top of each bottom bun half. Combine the butter and Kitchen Bouquet in a bowl and mix well. Spread over each patty. Place a slice of bacon on top. Place on a baking sheet.
- Bake at 425 degrees for 20 minutes. Place the top bun half on each mushroom burger.
- *Yield: 6 servings*

Michael's Grilled Leg of Lamb

1 (4- to 5-pound) butterflied
  leg of lamb
1 cup dry red wine
3/4 cup soy sauce
4 large garlic cloves, crushed

2 tablespoons Dijon mustard
1/2 teaspoon mint (optional)
1 tablespoon rosemary
1 tablespoon coarsely ground
  pepper

- Place the lamb in a glass dish or large sealable plastic bag. Combine the
  wine, soy sauce, garlic, mustard, mint, rosemary and pepper in a bowl and
  mix well. Pour over the lamb. Marinate, covered, for 6 hours or longer in
  the refrigerator. For maximum flavor marinate for 8 to 12 hours. Drain,
  discarding the marinade.
- Grill 4 inches from hot coals for 20 minutes on each side or until done to
  taste, checking after 30 minutes. Cut into thin slices.
- *Yield: 4 to 6 servings*

Leg of Lamb

1/2 cup dry sherry
1/2 cup currant jelly
1/2 cup ketchup
1/2 teaspoon marjoram

1 (5-pound) leg of lamb
Salt and pepper to taste
Parsley for garnish
Lemon wedges for garnish

- Combine the sherry, currant jelly, ketchup and marjoram in a small
  saucepan. Cook until the jelly is melted, stirring frequently.
- Sprinkle the lamb with salt and pepper. Place on a rack in a shallow
  roasting pan. Bake at 325 degrees for 1 hour. Bake an additional 1 1/2 to
  2 hours or to 175 degrees on a meat thermometer for medium, basting
  frequently with the sherry sauce. Place the lamb on a serving platter.
  Garnish with parsley and lemon wedges.
- *Yield: 6 to 8 servings*

When Mary Watson was President, the League was approached by the Catawba Mental Health Center to write a HUD housing grant. They wanted to build twenty apartments for the chronically mentally ill of our community that would allow these patients to live independently. A one million dollar grant was funded for the Carolina Place apartments located off Dave Lyle Boulevard.

—Mrs. Paul C. Watson, Jr. (Mary F.)

Slow-Cooker Barbecue

Mrs. Paul C. Watson, Jr. (Mary F.), Past President, 1990–1991

1 (4-pound) Boston butt pork roast	1 teaspoon dry mustard
1 cup cider vinegar	1 tablespoon sugar
1 garlic clove, crushed	1/2 cup ketchup
4 to 6 drops Tabasco sauce	1 teaspoon salt
	1/4 teaspoon pepper

- Place the pork in the slow cooker. Combine the vinegar, garlic, Tabasco sauce, dry mustard, sugar, ketchup, salt and pepper in a bowl and mix well. Pour over the pork. Cook on High for 4 hours or until tender.
- Drain the cooked pork, reserving the sauce. Chop the pork finely. Serve with the reserved sauce.
- *Yield: 8 to 10 servings*

Bourbon Pork Tenderloins

1/4 cup bourbon	3 garlic cloves, minced
1/4 cup soy sauce	1/4 teaspoon ground ginger
1/4 cup packed brown sugar	1 teaspoon Worcestershire sauce
1/4 cup Dijon mustard	2 (1-pound) pork tenderloins
1/4 cup vegetable oil	

- Combine the bourbon, soy sauce, brown sugar, mustard, oil, garlic, ginger and Worcestershire sauce in a bowl and mix well. Combine with the pork tenderloins in a sealable plastic bag. Marinate, in the refrigerator, for 24 hours or longer; drain. Grill over hot coals for 25 minutes or to 160 degrees on a meat thermometer.
- *Yield: 4 to 6 servings*

Herb-Crusted Pork Tenderloins with Horseradish Roasted New Potatoes

2 pounds new potatoes

1/4 cup (1/2 stick) butter or margarine, melted

2 tablespoons horseradish

1/2 teaspoon salt

1/2 teaspoon freshly ground pepper

1/2 cup fine dry bread crumbs

1/3 cup chopped fresh basil

3 tablespoons olive oil

1 tablespoon freshly ground pepper

1 teaspoon kosher salt

3 tablespoons chopped fresh thyme

1 1/2 pounds pork tenderloins

2 tablespoons chopped fresh parsley

Fresh herb sprigs for garnish

- Peel a 1-inch strip around the center of each potato. Combine the potatoes, butter, horseradish, salt and 1/2 teaspoon pepper in a large bowl and toss gently. Place the potatoes on a lightly greased rack in a broiler pan. Bake at 425 degrees for 20 minutes.

- Combine the bread crumbs, basil, olive oil, 1 tablespoon pepper, kosher salt and thyme in a bowl and mix well. Moisten the tenderloins with water. Press the bread crumb mixture over the tenderloins. Place on the rack with the potatoes.

- Bake at 425 degrees for 25 minutes or until potatoes are tender and pork registers 160 degrees on a meat thermometer. Sprinkle the potatoes with the parsley. Slice the tenderloins. Arrange the potatoes and sliced tenderloins on a serving platter. Garnish with fresh herb sprigs.

- *Yield: 4 to 6 servings*

"Come See Me" is Rock Hill's annual spring festival that invites everyone to come out and "see" your friends and neighbors. Many activities are planned and one of the most popular is the fireworks show. Rock Hillians gather at the Winthrop Coliseum to share food and good times and watch fireworks explode over Winthrop Lake.

Honey-Grilled Pork Tenderloin
   Sandwiches

Artichoke Nibbles

Spinach and Artichoke Casserole

World's Best Cookies

Lemon Bars

Honey-Grilled Pork Tenderloins

2 or 3 (12-ounce) pork tenderloins
1/3 cup low-sodium soy sauce
1/2 teaspoon ground ginger
5 garlic cloves, cut into halves
2 tablespoons brown sugar
3 tablespoons honey
2 teaspoons dark sesame oil

- Trim the fat from the tenderloins. Make a lengthwise cut in each tenderloin, starting and stopping 1/4 inch from the ends. Place in a shallow container or sealable plastic bag. Combine the soy sauce, ginger, and garlic in a bowl and mix well. Pour over the tenderloins. Marinate, in the refrigerator, for 3 hours or longer, turning occasionally; drain.
- Combine the brown sugar, honey and sesame oil in a small saucepan. Cook until the brown sugar dissolves, stirring constantly.
- Place the tenderloins on a grill rack coated with nonstick cooking spray. Grill over medium-hot coals for 20 minutes, basting with the warm honey mixture frequently.
- *Yield: 6 servings*

Pork Tenderloins with Peanut Marinade

2 (12-ounce) pork tenderloins
1/2 cup vegetable oil
1/4 cup soy sauce
3 tablespoons chopped peanuts
2 tablespoons Worcestershire sauce
2 tablespoons chopped onion
3 garlic cloves, crushed
1 tablespoon brown sugar
1/2 teaspoon curry powder

- Place the tenderloins in a sealable plastic bag. Combine the oil, soy sauce, peanuts, Worcestershire sauce, onion, garlic, brown sugar and curry powder in a bowl and mix well. Pour over the tenderloins. Marinate, in the refrigerator, for 3 hours or longer; drain.
- Place the tenderloins on a lightly greased rack in a broiler pan.
- Bake at 425 degrees for 20 minutes or until the tenderloins register 160 degrees on a meat thermometer.
- *Yield: 4 to 6 servings*

Pork with Peking Sauce

3 tablespoons cornstarch

3 tablespoons soy sauce

3 tablespoons sherry

3 pounds pork, sliced

1/4 cup cornstarch

1 tablespoon brown sugar

1 tablespoon vinegar

1 teaspoon salt

6 tablespoons hoisin sauce

1/4 cup soy sauce

3/4 cup chicken broth

6 tablespoons vegetable oil

3 garlic cloves, minced

3 teaspoons minced gingerroot

3 tablespoons vegetable oil

1 bunch broccoli, chopped

9 green onions, sliced diagonally

1 (8-ounce) can bamboo shoots, drained

2 (15-ounce) cans baby corn, drained

1 (8-ounce) can water chestnuts, drained

- Combine 3 tablespoons cornstarch, 3 tablespoons soy sauce and sherry in a large bowl and mix well. Add the pork, stirring to coat.
- Combine 1/4 cup cornstarch, brown sugar, vinegar, salt, hoisin sauce, 1/4 cup soy sauce and broth in a bowl and mix well. Set aside.
- Heat 6 tablespoons oil in a wok. Stir-fry the garlic and gingerroot in the hot oil. Add the pork mixture. Cook for 5 minutes. Remove the pork and set aside, keeping warm.
- Add 3 tablespoons oil to the wok. Add the broccoli and stir-fry for 2 minutes. Add the green onions and stir-fry for 2 minutes. Add the bamboo shoots, baby corn and water chestnuts and stir-fry for 2 minutes. Add the pork and the hoisin mixture. Cook until thickened, stirring constantly.
- *Yield: 8 to 12 servings*

Pork Chop Casserole

3/4 cup flour

1 teaspoon salt

1/2 teaspoon pepper

6 (3/4- to 1-inch-thick) pork chops

2 tablespoons vegetable oil

1 (10-ounce) can cream of mushroom soup

2/3 cup chicken broth

1/2 teaspoon ground ginger

1/4 teaspoon rosemary

1 cup sour cream

1 (3-ounce) can French-fried onions

- Combine the flour, salt and pepper in a shallow dish and mix well. Dredge the pork chops in the flour mixture. Heat the oil in a large skillet. Add the pork chops. Cook for 4 to 5 minutes on each side or until browned. Arrange in a single layer in a 9×13-inch baking dish.
- Combine the soup, broth, ginger, rosemary and 1/2 cup of the sour cream in a bowl and mix well. Pour over the chops. Sprinkle with half of the onions.
- Bake, covered, at 350 degrees for 45 to 50 minutes. Stir in the remaining 1/2 cup sour cream. Sprinkle the remaining onions over the top. Bake for an additional 10 minutes.
- *Yield: 6 servings*

Pork Chops with Caramelized Onions

2 tablespoons butter or roasted
   garlic butter
4 (1/2-inch-thick) pork chops
1/2 teaspoon salt

1/2 teaspoon pepper
3 medium onions, thinly sliced
1/2 teaspoon thyme

- Heat the butter in a 10-inch skillet until melted and sizzling. Add the pork chops. Cook over medium-high heat for 8 to 10 minutes or until browned, turning once. Sprinkle with the salt and pepper. Remove the chops to a serving platter.
- Place the onions in the skillet. Sprinkle with the thyme. Cook for 8 to 10 minutes or until onions are caramelized, stirring occasionally.
- Add the cooked chops to the onions. Cook for 4 to 5 minutes or until heated through.
- *Yield: 4 servings*

Baked Ham in Beer

1/2 cup dry mustard
1 cup packed brown sugar
1 (8- to 10-pound) cooked ham

12 bay leaves
4 cups beer

- Combine the dry mustard and brown sugar in a bowl and mix well. Add enough water to make of a paste consistency. Spread over the ham. Attach the bay leaves with wooden picks onto the ham. Place in a roasting pan. Pour the beer around the ham. Bake, covered, at 350 degrees for 1 hour.
- *Yield: 16 servings*

Ham Tetrazzini

1 tablespoon margarine
1 cup diced ham
1 small onion, chopped
1 (10-ounce) can cream of mushroom soup
5 ounces water
1 tablespoon cooking sherry
1 cup shredded cheese
1 tablespoon parsley
1 tablespoon Worcestershire sauce
1 (2-ounce) jar pimentos
8 ounces spaghetti, cooked

- Heat the margarine in a large skillet until melted. Add the ham and onion. Sauté until the onion is tender. Stir in the soup, water, sherry and cheese. Cook until cheese is melted, stirring constantly. Stir the parsley, Worcestershire sauce and pimentos into the ham mixture.
- Spread the spaghetti over the bottom of a baking dish. Spoon the ham mixture evenly over the spaghetti. Bake at 350 degrees until heated through.
- *Yield: 2 servings*

ARTS IN THE SCHOOLS

In 1973 the Junior Welfare League sponsored a fine arts project by sending all fourth graders to see two performances at Winthrop. This was the beginning of the "Arts In The Schools" program. The Fine Arts Association, now ARTS etc., was included in the annual budget until it was well established and funded by other sources.

Roast Veal with Lemon and Capers

1 egg
1 egg yolk
2 teaspoons Dijon mustard
Grated zest of 3 lemons
Juice of 1 lemon
1 cup olive oil
1½ tablespoons capers, drained
1 teaspoon oregano
Salt and ground pepper to taste

1 (3½- to 4-pound) veal loin
    roast, boned, rolled, tied
4 slices bacon
4 garlic cloves
⅓ cup dry white wine
½ cup (1 stick) unsalted butter,
    softened
⅔ cup dry white wine

- Combine the egg, egg yolk, mustard, lemon zest and lemon juice in a food processor container fitted with a steel blade. Process for 10 seconds. Add the olive oil in a fine stream, processing constantly until smooth. Add the capers, oregano, salt and pepper and process for 10 seconds.
- Place the veal in a shallow roasting pan. Pour 1 cup of the olive oil mixture over the veal. Store the remaining olive oil mixture, covered, in the refrigerator until serving time. Wrap the bacon slices around the veal.
- Purée the garlic and ⅓ cup wine in a food processor container fitted with a steel blade. Sprinkle over the bacon. Place the butter on top; this will melt as the roast cooks.
- Bake at 375 degrees for 2½ hours, basting occasionally with the ⅔ cup wine and the pan juices. Cut the roast into slices. Arrange on a serving plate with the bacon. Serve with the reserved olive oil mixture.
- *Editor's Note:* In order to avoid raw eggs that may contain salmonella, pasteurize the egg yolk before using. Mix 1 egg yolk with 1 tablespoon lemon juice or vinegar and 1 tablespoon water in a small glass bowl. Microwave, covered, on High for 30 seconds or until the mixture begins to rise. Microwave for 5 seconds longer. Beat with a wire whisk until smooth. Microwave on High for 10 seconds or until the mixture rises again. Beat again. Mixture should be at 200 degrees. Cover the bowl and let stand for 1 minute before using.
- *Yield: 6 to 8 servings*

Veal Stroganoff

1 (2-pound) boneless veal roast
½ cup (1 stick) butter
Garlic salt to taste
½ cup dry white wine
1 (10-ounce) can cream of celery soup
Grated zest of 1 lemon
Juice of 1 lemon
1 cup sliced mushrooms
8 ounces fettuccini or medium egg noodles, cooked

- Cut the veal into ½-inch-thick slices. Heat the butter in a skillet until melted. Add the veal. Cook until browned. Sprinkle with the garlic salt. Add the wine, soup, lemon zest and lemon juice, stirring until blended.
- Bring the veal mixture to a boil. Stir in the mushrooms. Reduce the heat. Simmer for 30 minutes or until veal is tender. Serve over the hot cooked fettuccini.
- *Yield: 4 to 6 servings*

MEATS

JWL ANNUAL LUNCHEON

Since 1969 the Junior Welfare League has held its annual luncheon or dinner at the Rock Hill Country Club. The exception came in 1974 when the luncheon was held at Rambo Mansion. That year some of the sustainers decided to dress up for a day in the "Deep South," parasols and all, and ride to the mansion in a horse-drawn buggy. They arrived, however, on the back of a convertible because that morning the poor horse died.

Marvelous Marinade

1¹⁄₂ cups vegetable oil	¹⁄₂ cup wine vinegar
³⁄₄ cup soy sauce	4¹⁄₂ teaspoons chopped fresh
¹⁄₄ cup Worcestershire sauce	parsley, or 1¹⁄₂ teaspoons
2 tablespoons dry mustard	dried parsley
1 teaspoon pepper	¹⁄₃ cup lemon juice
1¹⁄₄ teaspoons salt	2 garlic cloves, minced

- Combine the oil, soy sauce, Worcestershire sauce, dry mustard, pepper, salt, vinegar, parsley, lemon juice and garlic in a bowl and mix well. Pour over steak, chicken or other meat of choice. Marinate, covered, in the refrigerator for 24 hours or longer.
- *Yield: 3¹⁄₂ cups*

Barbecue Sauce

5 or 6 (15-ounce) bottles hot	1 cup soy sauce
and spicy ketchup	¹⁄₄ cup mustard
1 (32-ounce) bottle lemon juice	Hot sauce to taste
1 cup Worcestershire sauce	Salt and pepper to taste
¹⁄₄ cup packed brown sugar	¹⁄₂ cup (1 stick) butter, melted
1 (2-ounce) bottle Kitchen	
Bouquet	

- Combine the ketchup, lemon juice, Worcestershire sauce, brown sugar, Kitchen Bouquet, soy sauce, mustard, hot sauce, salt, pepper and butter in a saucepan. Bring to a simmer. Cook until desired consistency. Let cool. Store, covered, in the refrigerator.
- *Yield: about 15 cups*

Poultry

Wholeness
Dottie Moore

Dottie Moore

Dottie Moore's tapestry is titled Wholeness. *Dottie's art quilts are conversations with the earth and sky, visually conveying quiet moments in nature.*

Dottie Moore, a Rock Hill resident, has been producing art quilts for individual and corporate clients since 1980, winning numerous awards and honors. Each piece is appliquéd, quilted, and hand-embroidered. Her work is collected, exhibited, and published internationally.

Cheesy Glazed Chicken

3 tablespoons flour
1 teaspoon paprika
1 teaspoon salt
6 skinless chicken breasts
2 tablespoons butter
1 tablespoon vegetable oil
1/4 cup dry sherry
1 teaspoon cornstarch
3/4 cup half-and-half
1/2 teaspoon salt
1/3 cup sauterne or chablis
1 tablespoon lemon juice
1/2 cup shredded Muenster cheese

- Combine the flour, paprika and 1 teaspoon salt in a sealable plastic bag and mix well. Add the chicken and shake until lightly coated.
- Heat the butter and oil in a large skillet over medium heat until butter is melted. Add the chicken. Cook until browned. Add the sherry. Cook, covered, for 25 minutes or until chicken is tender. Remove the chicken and arrange in an ovenproof serving dish. You may debone the chicken if desired.
- Combine the cornstarch, half-and-half and 1/2 teaspoon salt in a bowl and mix until smooth. Stir into the pan juices. Cook until thickened, stirring constantly. Stir in the sauterne and lemon juice. Cook until heated through. Pour over the chicken. Sprinkle the cheese over the top. Broil until the cheese is melted.
- *Yield: 6 servings*

Basil-Stuffed Chicken with Tomato Garlic Pasta

4 (4-ounce) boneless skinless
    chicken breast halves
1/4 teaspoon salt
1/4 teaspoon garlic powder
2 bunches fresh basil (about
    20 leaves)

12 ounces angel hair pasta
Tomato Garlic Pasta Sauce
    (page 127)
1 cup grated Parmesan or
    Romano cheese
Fresh basil sprigs for garnish

- Pound the chicken breasts 1/4 inch thick between sheets of plastic wrap. Sprinkle with the salt and garlic powder. Arrange the basil leaves in a single layer over the chicken. Roll up one chicken breast starting from the short end. Place the roll on top of another chicken breast and roll up, forming a large roll. Secure with wooden picks. Repeat with the two remaining chicken breasts.

- Grill, covered, over medium-hot coals for 18 to 20 minutes or until cooked through, turning once. Chill, wrapped in foil, for 8 to 12 hours.

- Cook the pasta using the package directions. Drain and keep warm.

- Place chicken rolls on a microwave-safe plate. Microwave, covered, on Medium for 1 1/2 minutes, turning once. Remove the wooden picks. Cut each roll into thin slices. Place the pasta in a large serving bowl. Arrange the chicken slices over the pasta. Spoon the Tomato Garlic Pasta Sauce (page 127) over the chicken. Sprinkle with the Parmesan cheese. Garnish with the basil sprigs.

- *Yield: 4 servings*

Tomato Garlic Pasta Sauce

20 garlic cloves, chopped
2 tablespoons olive oil
3 large tomatoes, peeled, seeded, chopped
1/2 cup chablis

1/4 cup fresh basil leaves, cut into 1/4-inch strips
3 to 4 tablespoons balsamic vinegar
1 teaspoon pepper

• Brown the garlic in the olive oil in a skillet over medium-high heat. Stir in the tomatoes, chablis, basil, balsamic vinegar and pepper. Cook until heated through.

Chicken and Wild Rice Dijon

1 (6-ounce) package long grain and wild rice
1 (2-ounce) jar pimentos, drained
12 boneless skinless chicken breast halves

Salt and pepper to taste
2 tablespoons butter
2 garlic cloves, minced
1 cup heavy cream
1 tablespoon Dijon mustard
1 tablespoon parsley

• Cook the rice using the package directions. Stir in the pimentos. Set aside, keeping warm.

• Season the chicken with salt and pepper. Heat the butter in a skillet until melted. Add the chicken. Cook over medium heat for 7 minutes or until chicken is tender. Remove the chicken and keep warm.

• Sauté the garlic lightly in the pan juices. Stir in the cream, mustard and parsley. Cook for 5 minutes or until thickened, stirring constantly.

• Spoon the rice onto a serving platter. Arrange the chicken over the rice. Spoon the sauce over the chicken.

• *Yield: 10 servings*

Chicken Alouette

1 (17-ounce) package frozen
    puff pastry sheets, thawed
1 (4-ounce) package Alouette
    cheese
6 boneless skinless chicken
    breast halves

$^1/_2$ teaspoon salt
$^1/_8$ teaspoon pepper
1 egg, beaten
1 tablespoon water
Kale for garnish

- Unfold the pastry sheets. Roll each sheet into a 12×14-inch rectangle on a lightly floured surface. Cut one sheet into four 6×7-inch rectangles. Cut the remaining sheet into two 6×7-inch rectangles and one 6×12-inch rectangle. Set the large rectangle aside. Shape each small rectangle into an oval, trimming off the corners. Spread the pastry ovals evenly with the cheese.
- Sprinkle the chicken with the salt and pepper. Place one chicken breast on each pastry oval. Moisten the pastry edges lightly with water. Fold the ends over the chicken. Fold the side over and press to seal. Place each bundle seam side down on a greased baking sheet.
- Cut the large pastry rectangle into $^1/_4$×12-inch strips. Braid two strips together and place crosswise over a chicken bundle, trimming the excess braid. Braid two strips together and place lengthwise over the bundle, trimming and tucking the ends of the excess braid under the bundle. Repeat with the remaining strips and chicken bundles. You may chill the chicken bundles, covered, for up to 2 hours.
- Combine the egg and water in a small bowl and mix well. Brush over the pastry bundles. Bake at 400 degrees on the lower oven rack for 25 minutes or until golden brown. Garnish with kale.
- *Yield: 6 servings*

Chicken Cacciatore

2 cups chopped tomatoes
1 (8-ounce) jar seasoned
    tomato sauce
1 teaspoon salt
1 teaspoon oregano
1/2 teaspoon celery salt

1/4 teaspoon pepper
2 bay leaves
6 to 8 chicken breasts
1/4 cup olive oil
2 medium onions, chopped
2 garlic cloves, minced

- Mix the tomatoes, tomato sauce, salt, oregano, celery salt, pepper and bay leaves in a bowl. Brown the chicken in the olive oil in a large skillet. Remove the chicken. Add the onions and garlic to the skillet. Cook until onions are tender. Add the chicken to the skillet. Pour the tomato mixture over the chicken. Simmer, covered, for 45 minutes.
- Cook, uncovered, for 20 minutes or until chicken is tender and sauce is of the desired consistency, turning the chicken occasionally. Skim the top and remove the bay leaves before serving.
- *Yield: 6 to 8 servings*

Chicken Casserole

1 cup sour cream
1 (10-ounce) can cream of
    chicken soup
1 chicken, cooked, boned,
    cut into large pieces
32 butter crackers, crushed

1/2 cup (1 stick) unsalted butter,
    melted
Poppy seeds to taste
Freshly grated Parmesan cheese
    for garnish
Fresh parsley for garnish

- Combine the sour cream and soup in a bowl and mix well. Fold in the chicken pieces. Spoon into a buttered baking dish.
- Combine the crackers, butter and poppy seeds in a bowl and mix well. Sprinkle over the chicken mixture. Bake at 350 degrees for 30 minutes or until bubbly. Garnish with Parmesan cheese and parsley.
- *Yield: 4 servings*

Chicken Sesame

6 boneless chicken breasts
³/₄ cup flour
1 egg
³/₄ cup milk
2 cups saltine crumbs
Vegetable oil for frying
1 cup (2 sticks) butter
3 cups milk
2 chicken bouillon cubes
¹/₄ teaspoon salt
¹/₈ teaspoon garlic salt
5 teaspoons cornstarch
¹/₂ cup cold water
1 head iceberg lettuce, chopped
1 to 2 tablespoons sesame seeds, toasted
1¹/₂ cups rice, cooked

- Cut the chicken into 1¹/₂-inch pieces. Dredge in the flour. Combine the egg and ³/₄ cup milk in a bowl and mix well. Dip the floured chicken pieces into the egg mixture. Roll in the cracker crumbs. Deep-fry in 375-degree oil until light brown.
- Heat the butter in a 2-quart saucepan until melted. Add 3 cups milk, bouillon cubes, salt and garlic salt. Bring to a boil, stirring constantly. Combine the cornstarch and water in a small bowl, stirring until smooth. Stir into the milk mixture. Cook until of the desired consistency, stirring constantly.
- Arrange the lettuce over the bottom of a deep serving plate. Arrange the chicken nuggets over the lettuce. Pour the hot sauce over the chicken. Sprinkle with sesame seeds. Serve over the rice.
- *Yield: 6 servings*

Chicken Tetrazzini

Mrs. Frederick William Faircloth III (Phyllis Hatfield),
Past President, 1987–1988

6 boneless skinless chicken breast halves
2 chicken bouillon cubes
3½ cups water
8 ounces mushrooms, sliced
5 tablespoons butter
¼ cup flour
2 cups half-and-half
7½ teaspoons dry sherry
1 cup chopped olives
8 ounces spaghetti, cooked
1 cup shredded sharp Cheddar cheese

- Combine the chicken, bouillon cubes and water in a saucepan. Bring to a boil. Reduce the heat. Simmer, covered, until chicken is tender. Drain, reserving the broth. Cool the chicken. Cut the chicken into bite-size pieces. Strain the broth.
- Sauté the mushrooms in the butter in a skillet. Stir in the flour. Add the half-and-half and 1 cup of the broth gradually, stirring constantly. Cook until of the desired consistency, whisking constantly. Stir in the chicken, sherry and olives.
- Spread the spaghetti over the bottom of a greased shallow baking dish. Spoon the chicken mixture over the spaghetti. Sprinkle the cheese over the top. Bake at 350 degrees for 30 minutes.
- *Yield: 6 to 8 servings*

SCHOLARSHIP FUNDS

The Rock Hill Junior Welfare League Scholarship Fund for Winthrop students was established in 1957. It began with a gift of a one-year scholarship for one girl that could be renewed each year. A four-year scholarship was added later.

Chicken with Lemon Sage Sauce

4 boneless skinless chicken breast halves

Salt and pepper to taste

$1/4$ cup flour

$1^1/2$ tablespoons butter

$1^1/2$ tablespoons vegetable oil

2 medium garlic cloves, thinly sliced

15 medium fresh whole sage leaves

2 tablespoons lemon juice

1 cup chicken stock

3 tablespoons butter, softened

$1^1/2$ ounces prosciutto or country ham, finely chopped

- Season the chicken with salt and pepper. Dredge in the flour. Heat $1^1/2$ tablespoons butter and oil in a skillet over high heat until hot and bubbly. Reduce the heat to medium-high. Add the chicken. Cook for 4 minutes. Turn the chicken. Cook for 4 minutes or until cooked through. Remove to an ovenproof plate. Cover with foil. Place in a 200-degree oven.
- Sauté the garlic and sage leaves in the pan juices over medium heat for 1 to 2 minutes or until garlic is fragrant and the sage is crisp. Add the lemon juice. Bring to a boil, scraping the bottom of the skillet with a wooden spoon. Add the chicken stock. Increase the temperature to medium-high. Bring to a boil. Boil for 8 minutes or until reduced to $1/4$ cup, stirring occasionally. Remove from the heat.
- Add 3 tablespoons butter and prosciutto to the hot sauce, stirring until butter is melted. Season with salt and pepper. Place the chicken on a serving platter. Spoon the sauce over the chicken.
- *Yield: 4 servings*

Lite Chicken Piccata

4 boneless skinless chicken breast halves

1/4 cup flour

1/4 teaspoon salt

1/4 teaspoon pepper

1 1/2 tablespoons margarine

1/4 cup lemon juice

2 teaspoons water-packed capers, drained

1/4 lemon, thinly sliced, for garnish

Chopped parsley for garnish

- Pound the chicken breasts 1/4 inch thick between sheets of waxed paper. Cut each breast into 2 or 3 pieces. Combine the flour, salt and pepper in a shallow dish and mix well. Dredge the chicken pieces in the flour mixture.
- Heat the margarine in a large skillet coated with nonstick cooking spray over medium heat until melted. Add the chicken. Cook for 3 to 4 minutes on each side or until golden brown. Remove the chicken and drain on paper towels. Arrange chicken on a serving platter and keep warm.
- Add the lemon juice and capers to the pan juices. Cook until heated through, stirring occasionally. Pour over the chicken. Garnish with lemon slices and chopped parsley.
- *Yield: 4 servings*

*Invite a few families for a
Sunday afternoon cookout.
Each family may bring a
dish or prepare the menu
listed below.*

Marinated Chicken Kabobs
Hamburgers with Barbecue Sauce
Curried Rice Salad
Grilled Corn with Cumin Scallion Butter
Macadamia Nut Chocolate Chip Cookies

Marinated Chicken Kabobs

3 boneless skinless chicken breast halves
3 tablespoons soy sauce
3 tablespoons Italian salad dressing
2 teaspoons sesame seeds
2 teaspoons lemon juice
$1/2$ teaspoon ground ginger
3 carrots, cut into $1^1/_2$- to 2-inch pieces
1 small green bell pepper, cut into eighths
1 onion, cut into eighths
8 cherry tomatoes

- Cut the chicken breasts into 1-inch pieces. Place in a shallow container. Combine the soy sauce, salad dressing, sesame seeds, lemon juice and ginger in a bowl and mix well. Pour over the chicken. Marinate, covered, in the refrigerator for 2 hours or longer.
- Bring enough water to cover the vegetables to a boil in a saucepan. Add the carrots. Boil for 3 minutes. Add the bell pepper and onion. Boil until partially cooked; drain.
- Drain the chicken, reserving the marinade. Place the reserved marinade in a small saucepan. Bring to a boil. Boil for 2 to 3 minutes, stirring constantly. Thread the chicken, carrots, bell pepper and onion alternately on 12-inch skewers, allowing room on the end for the tomatoes. Brush with the marinade.
- Grill the kabobs over hot coals until partially cooked, turning frequently. Thread the tomatoes onto the ends of the skewers. Grill until chicken is tender. You may broil or microwave the kabobs.
- *Yield: 6 servings*

Sesame Chicken with Celery

Mrs. James Wilson Johnston (Karen Rowe), Past President, 1995–1996

12 boneless skinless chicken breast halves
2 tablespoons dry sherry
2 tablespoons soy sauce
4 teaspoons grated gingerroot
1/2 cup chicken broth
2 teaspoons cornstarch
1/4 cup vegetable oil
6 celery ribs, cut diagonally
8 green onions, cut diagonally
1/4 cup sesame seeds, toasted

- Cut the chicken into 1-inch pieces. Place in a shallow container. Combine the sherry, soy sauce and gingerroot in a bowl and mix well. Pour over the chicken, stirring to coat. Set aside. Combine the chicken broth and cornstarch in a small bowl and mix well.

- Heat the wok over high heat. Add the oil. Stir-fry the celery and green onions for 2 minutes. Remove from the wok. Drain the chicken, reserving the marinade. Stir the marinade into the chicken broth mixture. Add the chicken to the wok. Stir-fry for 3 minutes or until brown.

- Pour the chicken broth mixture into the wok. Cook until thickened and bubbly, stirring constantly. Cook for 2 minutes. Stir in the cooked celery and green onions. Cook for 1 minute. Sprinkle with the sesame seeds. Serve immediately.

- *Yield: 8 to 12 servings*

POULTRY

MAY THE BEST WOK WIN

Past President Karen Johnston's favorite dinner party is more fun than a Chinese New Year! "I always fix the appetizers, soup, and dessert. We set up three or four wok stations with all the ingredients and utensils. Then we divide our guests into teams of four and ask each team to prepare one of the main dishes." Good-spirited competition ensues as the guests participate in the "cook-off." May the best wok win!

Napa Salad
Sesame Chicken with Celery
Pork with Peking Sauce
Kung Pao Seafood
Mongolian Beef

Army-Navy Chicken Curry with Chutney Peaches

6 small to medium chicken
   breast halves
1 cup coarsely chopped peanuts
1 (2-ounce) package raisins
8 ounces bacon, crisp-cooked,
   crumbled
2 (10-ounce) cans cream of
   chicken soup
1¼ cups applesauce

1 (12-ounce) jar chutney
2 tablespoons curry powder, or
   to taste
1 (4-ounce) can flaked coconut
1 (3-ounce) can French-fried
   onions
Chutney Peaches
Hot cooked white rice

- Combine the chicken with enough water to cover in a saucepan. Bring to a boil. Reduce the heat. Simmer just until chicken is tender; drain. Cut into bite-size pieces. Combine with the peanuts, raisins and bacon in a bowl and mix well.
- Combine the soup, applesauce, chutney and curry powder in a separate bowl and mix well. Add the chicken mixture, tossing to coat. Spoon into a 9×12-inch baking dish. Sprinkle the coconut over the chicken mixture. Sprinkle the French-fried onions over the top.
- Bake at 325 degrees for 30 minutes or until heated through. Serve with the Chutney Peaches and rice.
- *Yield: 8 to 10 servings*

Chutney Peaches

1 (16-ounce) can peach halves
Chutney

Butter
Brown sugar

- Arrange the peach halves in a baking dish. Fill the center of each peach half with chutney. Dot with a small amount of butter. Sprinkle with brown sugar. Bake at 325 degrees for 10 minutes or until heated through.

Chicken Fajitas

1/4 cup orange juice

1/4 cup pineapple juice

1 teaspoon oregano

1 teaspoon cumin

1 teaspoon chili powder

3 garlic cloves, chopped

1 teaspoon salt, or to taste

1/2 teaspoon pepper, or to taste

1 1/2 pounds chicken, cut into strips

1 tablespoon olive oil

12 ounces onions, sliced

1 1/2 large red bell peppers, cut into strips

1 1/2 large green bell peppers, cut into strips

3 garlic cloves, chopped

3/4 cup salsa

8 corn tortillas

- Combine the orange juice, pineapple juice, oregano, cumin, chili powder, 3 garlic cloves, salt and pepper in a shallow dish and mix well. Add the chicken and toss to coat. Marinate, in the refrigerator, for 30 minutes; drain.
- Place the chicken on a rack in a broiler pan. Broil for 2 minutes on each side or until tender. Set aside and keep warm. Heat the olive oil in a skillet. Add the onions, bell peppers and 3 garlic cloves. Cook for 15 minutes, stirring frequently. Add the salsa and mix well. Cook until heated through.
- Wrap the tortillas in foil. Bake at 350 degrees for 10 minutes or until warm. Serve with the cooked chicken and salsa mixture.
- *Yield: 4 servings*

Double-Crust Chicken Potpie

2 tablespoons butter or
    margarine, melted
6 boneless skinless chicken
    breasts, cut into 1-inch pieces
1 medium onion, chopped
1 cup sliced fresh mushrooms
³/₄ cup chopped carrots
1 rib celery, chopped
³/₄ cup frozen English peas
³/₄ cup cubed potatoes
1 cup chicken broth
¹/₄ cup chablis or other dry
    white wine
¹/₂ teaspoon parsley

¹/₄ teaspoon white pepper
1 bay leaf
2 tablespoons cornstarch
2 tablespoons water
1 (10-ounce) can cream of
    mushroom or cream of
    chicken soup
¹/₂ cup sour cream
³/₄ cup shredded Cheddar cheese
1 (2-crust) pie pastry
1 egg yolk, lightly beaten
1 tablespoon half-and-half or
    milk

- Heat the butter in a large skillet until melted. Add the chicken and onion. Sauté for 5 minutes. Add the mushrooms, carrots, celery, peas, potatoes, broth, chablis, parsley, white pepper and bay leaf and mix well. Bring to a boil. Reduce the heat. Simmer, covered, for 15 minutes or until vegetables are tender. Remove the bay leaf.
- Combine the cornstarch and water in a small bowl and mix until smooth. Add to the chicken mixture. Bring to a boil over medium heat, stirring constantly. Remove from the heat. Stir in the soup, sour cream and cheese.
- Fit one of the pie pastries into a pie plate. Spoon the chicken mixture into the pastry-lined pie plate. Top with the remaining pastry, sealing and fluting the edge and cutting vents. Combine the egg yolk and half-and-half in a small bowl and mix well. Brush over the pastry.
- Bake at 400 degrees for 30 minutes, covering with foil as needed to prevent excessive browning.
- *Yield: 6 servings*

Duck Shish Kabobs

4 duck breast halves, boned, skinned
1 (16-ounce) can pineapple chunks
1 (8-ounce) bottle Italian salad dressing
1 (6-ounce) can frozen orange juice concentrate
²/₃ cup Worcestershire sauce
12 cherry tomatoes
1 green bell pepper, cut into 12 squares
12 fresh mushrooms

- Cut each duck breast into 3 lengthwise strips. Arrange the strips in a shallow dish. Drain the pineapple, reserving the juice. Combine the reserved pineapple juice and salad dressing in a bowl and mix well. Pour over the duck.
- Marinate, covered, in the refrigerator for 3 hours or longer. Drain, reserving the marinade. Combine the reserved marinade, orange juice concentrate and Worcestershire sauce in a saucepan. Bring to a boil. Reduce the heat. Simmer for 5 minutes.
- Thread 1 piece duck, 1 pineapple chunk, 1 cherry tomato, 1 square bell pepper and 1 mushroom onto each of 12 skewers. Grill over medium-hot coals for 15 to 20 minutes or until the duck is tender, turning and basting frequently with the marinade mixture. Serve the remaining marinade mixture with the kabobs.
- *Yield: 6 servings*

QUOTE

America is woven of many strands—Our fate is to become one and yet many.

—Ralph Ellison

HUNT CLUB SUPPER

Whenever Harry Hicklin has a freezer full of game, he invites his hunting buddies and their wives for dinner. Leila brings in table decorations from the wild, her own backyard. An artful arrangement of twigs, leaves, and pinecones sets the mood. Rustic pottery and lanterns complete the earthy feel of the table setting. After dinner, cigars for the gentlemen and tall tales about "the one that got away" are a must!

Duck Shish Kabobs

Grilled Quail with Red Wine
  Blackberry Sauce

Posh Squash

Mexican Corn Muffins

Hot Fruit Compote

Tiramisu

Grilled Quail with Red Wine Blackberry Sauce

2 (14-ounce) packages quail, dressed, with breasts deboned
1 (8-ounce) bottle Italian salad dressing
½ cup dry red wine
1 (9-ounce) jar seedless blackberry spread

- Rinse and pat dry the quail. Place in a large shallow dish. Pour the salad dressing over the quail. Marinate, covered, in the refrigerator for 8 hours, turning occasionally; drain.
- Cook the wine in a small saucepan over medium heat for 5 minutes or until reduced by half. Whisk in the blackberry spread until smooth; reserve ¾ cup.
- Grill the quail over medium, 300- to 350-degree, coals for 15 minutes, turning once and basting with the remaining blackberry sauce. Serve with the reserved blackberry sauce.
- *Yield: 4 servings*

*Loaves and Fishes/
Having it All*
Marie Holbert Aycock

Seafood

Marie Holbert Aycock

Marie Holbert Aycock's painting, Loaves and Fishes/ Having it All, *speaks of the creative nature of women as a whole. Whether preparing a meal or giving birth to a child, women participate in the miracles of everyday life.*

Marie Holbert Aycock, a Rock Hill resident and mother to four school-aged sons, currently paints in mixed watercolor media. Marie's work has won many awards, and can be seen in private and corporate collections throughout the Carolinas as well as other states.

Crawfish Étouffée

Sandra Thomas, Past President, 1989–1990

½ cup (1 stick) butter
1 cup finely chopped onion
1 cup finely chopped celery
½ cup finely chopped
   green onions
¼ cup chopped shallots
2 garlic cloves, mashed
2 tablespoons flour
2 cups chicken stock or broth
1 (15-ounce) can Rotel tomatoes
Salt to taste

1 teaspoon freshly ground
   black pepper
Dash of cayenne pepper
1 tablespoon Worcestershire
   sauce
2 pounds crawfish meat or
   shrimp
Cornstarch for thickening
   (optional)
3 cups hot cooked white rice

- Heat the butter in a heavy Dutch oven over medium heat until melted. Add the onion, celery, green onions, shallots and garlic. Sauté until tender; do not brown. Add the flour. Cook until brown, stirring constantly. Add the chicken stock gradually, stirring constantly. Add the tomatoes and mix well. Simmer for 10 minutes.

- Add salt, black pepper, cayenne pepper and Worcestershire sauce to the tomato mixture and mix well. Adjust the seasonings to make spicy. Rinse lightly and drain the crawfish if it was frozen. Stir the crawfish into the étoufée. Cook over low heat for 15 minutes.

- Add the cornstarch to a small amount of cold water, stirring until dissolved. Stir into the étouffée. Cook until of the desired consistency, stirring constantly. Serve over the rice.

- *Yield: 6 to 8 servings*

Years ago my two sons' recipes were published in the Junior Welfare League children's cookbook. Today my sons are thirty and thirty-one years old and have a lot of fun when the cookbook is mentioned and we read the recipes. Jeff lives in Rock Hill, and his wife, Julia, is now a League member. So the tradition goes on.

My husband's mother, Nanee Pilcher, was also a President of the League. What I know about cooking, I learned from Nanee and my mother Mamie Ogburn. This recipe was handed down to me.

—Mrs. Thomas G. Pilcher (Linda Ogburn)

Oysters Rockefeller

Mrs. Thomas G. Pilcher (Linda Ogburn), Past President, 1981–1982

3 dozen oysters and shells
1/2 (10-ounce) package frozen chopped spinach, thawed
1/2 cup chopped fresh parsley
1/2 cup chopped scallions
1/2 cup torn Boston lettuce
1 garlic clove
1/2 cup (1 stick) butter, softened
3/4 cup bread crumbs
1 tablespoon Worcestershire sauce
1 teaspoon anchovy paste
4 drops of Tabasco sauce
1 1/2 tablespoons Pernod
1/2 teaspoon salt
1/4 cup grated Parmesan cheese
1/4 cup bread crumbs
Rock salt

- Preheat the oven to 450 degrees. Drain the oysters, reserving the liquid. Place the oysters in the shells.
- Combine the reserved oyster liquid, spinach, parsley, scallions, lettuce and garlic in a blender container and process. Add the butter and 3/4 cup bread crumbs and process. Add the Worcestershire sauce, anchovy paste, Tabasco sauce, Pernod and 1/2 teaspoon salt and process until well blended. Place a spoonful over each oyster.
- Sprinkle the Parmesan cheese over the sauce. Sprinkle 1/4 cup bread crumbs over the Parmesan cheese. Spread rock salt in a baking dish. Arrange the oysters on the rock salt. Bake for 20 minutes.
- *Yield: 6 servings*

Herbed Shrimp and Pasta

1 red bell pepper
2 small yellow squash
12 asparagus spears
8 ounces fresh mushrooms
6 garlic cloves, minced
2 large shallots, finely chopped
2 teaspoons olive oil
1 pound shrimp, peeled
2 plum tomatoes, chopped
1/2 teaspoon salt
1/4 teaspoon pepper
1/2 cup chopped parsley
1/4 cup chopped basil
1 tablespoon chopped thyme
10 ounces angel hair pasta, cooked, hot
1/2 cup grated Parmesan cheese

- Cut the bell pepper into thin strips. Cut the squash into halves. Cut each half into slices. Trim the asparagus and cut into 2-inch pieces. Slice the mushrooms.
- Sauté the garlic and shallots in the olive oil in a skillet until tender. Add the bell pepper, squash, asparagus and mushrooms. Sauté for 7 minutes or until tender-crisp. Add the shrimp. Sauté for 3 to 5 minutes or until the shrimp turn pink.
- Stir the tomatoes, salt, pepper, parsley, basil and thyme into the shrimp mixture. Cook until heated through.
- Combine the shrimp mixture and pasta in a large bowl and toss to combine. Sprinkle with the cheese.
- *Yield: 4 to 6 servings*

*Dig out your old Bob Marley
CDs, launch the pontoon
boat, and spend the afternoon
on the Caribbean Sea. Well,
not exactly. But with this
menu, a few good friends,
and a cool breeze, who will
notice? The prawns, pork
tenderloin, and red rice can
be served at room temperature
while the salad and dessert
should be chilled. Don't
Worry, Be Happy!*

Lime Prawns with Papaya Salsa
Pork Tenderloins with Peanut Marinade
Savannah Red Rice
Grape Tomato Salad
Lemon Bars

Lime Prawns with Papaya Salsa

16 prawns or jumbo shrimp
Juice of 3 limes
4 garlic cloves, finely minced
1 tablespoon olive oil

Freshly ground pepper
4 limes, cut into wedges
Papaya Salsa

- Arrange the prawns in a single layer in a shallow glass dish. Combine the lime juice, garlic, olive oil and pepper in a bowl and mix well. Pour over the prawns. Marinate, covered, in the refrigerator for 2 hours.
- Drain the prawns, reserving the marinade. Place the reserved marinade in a small saucepan. Bring to a boil. Boil for 2 to 3 minutes, stirring constantly.
- Thread the prawns on skewers. Place on a grill over hot coals. Grill for 10 minutes or until the prawns turn pink, turning and basting frequently with the reserved marinade.
- Remove the skewers from the prawns. Arrange the prawns on a serving platter. Garnish with the lime wedges. Serve with the Papaya Salsa.
- *Yield: 4 servings*

Papaya Salsa

2 papayas (about 1 pound)
1 jalapeño chile
**1 large garlic clove, finely
   minced**

1/2 cup finely chopped red onion
1/4 cup coarsely chopped cilantro
Grated zest of 2 limes
1/2 cup fresh lime juice

- Peel the papayas and cut into 1/4- to 1/2-inch cubes. Place in a bowl. Seed and finely chop the jalapeño pepper. Combine the jalapeño pepper, garlic, onion, cilantro, lime zest and lime juice with the papaya and toss gently to combine. Serve within 6 hours for the freshest taste.

Shrimp Edisto

12 ounces vermicelli

6 tablespoons (³/4 stick) butter

8 ounces fresh mushrooms, sliced

1 cup chopped onion

6 tablespoons (³/4 stick) butter

2 pounds small shrimp, peeled, deveined

1 teaspoon salt

¹/2 teaspoon lemon pepper

2 tablespoons chopped parsley

1 tablespoon Worcestershire sauce

4 ounces chopped black olives

¹/2 cup grated Romano cheese

- Cook the vermicelli using the package directions until al dente; drain.
- Heat 6 tablespoons butter in a saucepan over medium heat until melted. Add the mushrooms and onion. Sauté for 5 to 8 minutes or until tender. Spoon into a large bowl.
- Heat 6 tablespoons butter in the same saucepan until melted. Add the shrimp. Cook just until pink. Add to the mushroom mixture. Add the salt, lemon pepper, parsley, Worcestershire sauce, olives and ¹/4 cup of the Romano cheese and mix well. Add the cooked vermicelli and mix well.
- Spoon into a 9×13-inch baking dish. Sprinkle with the remaining ¹/4 cup cheese. Bake at 350 degrees for 20 to 30 minutes or until heated through. Chill for 3 or more hours and reheat for maximum flavor.
- *Yield: 6 to 8 servings*

Shrimp and Fettuccini

1/2 cup (1 stick) butter, softened
8 ounces mushrooms, sliced
2 bunches green onions, chopped
1 garlic clove, minced
1 pound shrimp, peeled, deveined
Flour for coating
3/4 cup white wine
1 tablespoon lemon juice
1/4 to 1/2 teaspoon cayenne pepper
1/4 teaspoon paprika
1/4 teaspoon thyme
1/4 teaspoon oregano
Salt to taste
1 to 1 1/2 cups half-and-half
8 ounces fettuccini, cooked
1/2 cup chopped fresh parsley

- Heat the butter in a large skillet until melted. Add the mushrooms, green onions and garlic. Sauté until tender.
- Coat the shrimp lightly with flour. Add the shrimp and wine to the mushroom mixture and mix well. Cook for 3 minutes or until the shrimp turn pink. Stir in the lemon juice, cayenne pepper, paprika, thyme, oregano, salt and enough half-and-half to make of the desired consistency. Add the fettuccini. Cook until heated through, stirring frequently. Stir in the parsley.
- *Yield: 4 servings*

Shrimp and Grits

5 slices bacon
3 or 4 spring onions, chopped
1 to 2 tablespoons flour
1½ pounds shrimp, peeled, deveined
2 to 3 teaspoons Worcestershire sauce
1 cup water
Salt and pepper to taste
3 cups hot cooked grits

- Cook the bacon in a large skillet until crisp. Remove from the skillet and place on paper towels to drain. Drain the skillet, reserving half the drippings in the skillet.
- Add the spring onions to the hot drippings. Sauté over high heat until tender. Sprinkle the flour over the spring onions, stirring to combine. Reduce the heat to medium. Add the shrimp, Worcestershire sauce and water and mix well. Simmer for 2 to 3 minutes. Season with salt and pepper.
- Place the hot cooked grits in a serving bowl. Spoon the shrimp mixture over the grits. Crumble the bacon over the top.
- *Yield: 4 to 6 servings*

SEAFOOD

MIDNIGHT BREAKFAST AFTER THE HOLLY BALL

This is a wonderful way to entertain hungry teenagers after a night of dancing at Junior Assembly. Serve the breakfast buffet style and have tables set for your expected guests. Floating candles in large glass bowls and Christmas greenery make easy centerpieces. And do not forget the stars. It is, after all, midnight. Different shapes of star ornaments nestled in the greenery add sparkle to the table.

Holly Punch
Shrimp and Grits
Scrambled Eggs for a Crowd
Grilled Bacon for a Crowd
Martha's "Meant to Be" Cheese Danish
Fresh Fruit Plate

Shrimp Harpin

Mrs. H. B. Hilton (Rosa Wilder), Past President, 1951–1952

Shrimp Harpin has become a tradition in our family for Christmas dinner. It is served along with the Christmas ham, sweet potato or squash casserole, and a congealed salad.

Every year I think that I will vary the menu, but if I mention omitting the Shrimp Harpin there is much complaint.

—Mrs. H. B. Hilton (Rosa Wilder)

2 pounds large or medium shrimp, peeled, deveined, cooked
1 tablespoon lemon juice
3 tablespoons vegetable oil
3/4 cup rice
2 tablespoons butter or margarine
1/4 cup minced green bell pepper
1/4 cup minced onion
1 (10-ounce) can tomato soup
1/2 cup sherry
1 teaspoon salt
1/8 teaspoon black pepper
1/8 teaspoon mace
Dash of red pepper
1/2 cup sliced almonds
Paprika

- Arrange the shrimp in a shallow flat dish. Sprinkle with lemon juice. Sprinkle with the oil. Chill, covered, for 8 to 12 hours.
- Cook the rice using the package directions. Heat the butter in a saucepan until melted. Add the bell pepper and onion. Sauté until tender.
- Combine the soup, sherry, salt, black pepper, mace and red pepper in a large bowl and mix well. Add the shrimp, cooked rice, and bell pepper mixture and mix well. Spoon into a baking dish. Sprinkle the almonds and paprika over the top. Bake at 350 degrees for 55 minutes.
- *Yield: 8 servings*

Shrimp Sauce Piquant

3 tablespoons minced jalapeño
   peppers, or to taste
2 tablespoons unsalted butter
2¼ cups chopped onions
1½ cups chopped green
   bell peppers
¾ cup chopped celery
3 cups chopped peeled tomatoes
1 cup tomato sauce
2 bay leaves

5½ teaspoons cayenne pepper
1½ teaspoons white pepper
1 teaspoon black pepper
1½ teaspoons minced garlic
2¼ cups seafood stock
1½ tablespoons dark
   brown sugar
¾ teaspoon salt
2 pounds peeled large shrimp
4 cups hot cooked rice

- Rinse the jalapeño peppers thoroughly and pat dry if they are not fresh. Heat the butter in a 4-quart saucepan over high heat until melted. Add the onions, bell peppers and celery. Sauté for 2 minutes, stirring occasionally. Add the jalapeño peppers, tomatoes, tomato sauce, bay leaves, cayenne pepper, white pepper, black pepper and garlic and mix well. Cook for 3 minutes, stirring frequently and scraping the pan bottom.
- Stir the stock, brown sugar and salt into the tomato mixture. Bring to a boil. Reduce the heat. Simmer for 20 minutes, stirring frequently and scraping the pan bottom as needed. Chill, covered, for 1 day for maximum flavor.
- Stir the shrimp into the hot sauce. Increase the heat to high. Cook, covered, until the mixture boils. Remove from the heat. Let stand for 10 minutes. Remove the bay leaves.
- Mound ½ cup of the rice on each of 8 heated dinner plates. Pour ½ cup of the sauce around each rice mound. Arrange about 8 shrimp on top of the sauce.
- *Yield: 8 servings*

Shrimp with Tomatoes, Oregano and Feta

Salt and pepper to taste
1½ pounds large shrimp, peeled, deveined
4 tablespoons olive oil
1 small yellow onion, chopped
4 garlic cloves, finely minced
2 tablespoons oregano
1½ cups tomato sauce
8 ounces feta cheese, crumbled

- Sprinkle the salt and pepper over the shrimp. Heat 2 tablespoons of the olive oil in a skillet over medium heat. Add the shrimp. Sauté for 2 to 3 minutes or until the shrimp turn pink. Remove with a slotted spoon and arrange evenly over the bottom of a baking dish.
- Heat the remaining 2 tablespoons olive oil in the same skillet over medium heat. Add the onion. Sauté for 8 minutes or until tender. Add the garlic and oregano. Sauté for 2 minutes. Add the tomato sauce. Simmer for 2 minutes or until slightly thickened, stirring frequently. Season with salt and pepper.
- Pour the sauce over the shrimp. Sprinkle the feta cheese over the top. Bake at 450 degrees for 5 to 8 minutes or until the cheese melts. You may prepare up to 4 hours in advance prior to the addition of feta cheese. Bake at 450 degrees for 5 to 8 minutes or until the cheese melts and dish is heated through.
- *Yield: 4 servings*

Shrimp with Wild Rice

Mrs. John D. Good III (Vivienne Price), Past President, 1979–1980

½ cup (1 stick) butter
½ cup flour
4 cups chicken broth
¼ teaspoon white pepper
½ cup (1 stick) butter
1 cup thinly sliced onion
½ cup thinly sliced green bell pepper
1 cup thinly sliced mushrooms
2 pounds cooked peeled shrimp
2 tablespoons Worcestershire sauce
4 cups cooked long grain and wild rice

- Heat ½ cup butter in a skillet until melted. Stir in the flour gradually. Cook over low heat until bubbly, stirring constantly. Whisk in the broth gradually. Cook until smooth and thickened, stirring constantly. Stir in the white pepper. Simmer for 2 to 3 minutes, stirring constantly. Remove from the heat.
- Heat ½ cup butter in a separate skillet until melted. Add the onion, bell pepper and mushrooms. Sauté until tender; drain.
- Combine the sauce, cooked vegetables, shrimp, Worcestershire sauce and rice in a large bowl and mix well. Spoon into 2 shallow 2-quart baking dishes sprayed with nonstick cooking spray. Bake at 325 degrees for 45 to 50 minutes or until bubbly.
- *Yield: 8 to 12 servings*

SEAFOOD

PAST PRESIDENTS

It was customary for the president to have a luncheon for her board at the end of the year. This was the first year the board began night meetings. So, I served the "President's Board Dinner," and Shrimp with Wild Rice was the entrée. The menu was published in the League Lites.

—Mrs. John D. Good III (Vivienne Price)

As a Louisiana transplant, I cook far more gumbo and jambalaya since I have moved from New Orleans to Rock Hill ten years ago. When Mother comes to visit, she brings up fresh crawfish, andouille sausage, and other ingredients from Louisiana. People here just enjoy my Creole and Cajun dishes so much. And that's what cooks love to do—please people.

—Mrs. William G. McCarthy (Sheila)

Seafood Jambalaya

$2^{1}\!/_{2}$ cups (about) converted rice
1 (1-pound) package kielbasa sausage
1 medium onion, chopped
$^{1}\!/_{2}$ green bell pepper, chopped
2 ribs celery, chopped
2 garlic cloves, minced
2 tablespoons minced fresh parsley
4 ounces tomato paste
3 tablespoons water
$^{1}\!/_{4}$ teaspoon chili powder
$^{1}\!/_{4}$ teaspoon paprika
$1^{1}\!/_{2}$ pounds shrimp, peeled
Salt and pepper to taste

- Cook the rice using the package directions. Let stand until cool.
- Slice the kielbasa sausage. Brown in a Dutch oven over medium heat, stirring frequently. Add the onion, bell pepper and celery. Cook until tender, stirring constantly and scraping the pan bottom. Add the garlic. Cook until tender, stirring frequently. Add the parsley, tomato paste, water, chili powder and paprika and mix well. Cook for 5 minutes.
- Add the shrimp to the sausage mixture. Cook for 5 to 8 minutes or until the shrimp turn pink. Add the rice by cupfuls until the mixture is moist and not soupy, mixing well after each addition. Reserve any remaining rice for another use. Season with salt and pepper.
- *Yield: 6 to 8 servings*

Kung Pao Seafood

2 pounds shrimp, peeled,
  deveined

1 pound crab meat

8 ounces scallops

1/4 cup sherry

1/2 teaspoon salt

1/8 teaspoon white pepper

6 tablespoons soy sauce

3 tablespoons white vinegar

3 tablespoons sherry

1/2 cup chicken broth

2 tablespoons brown sugar

1/4 cup cornstarch

6 tablespoons vegetable oil

12 hot chile peppers

2 cups cashews

4 tablespoons vegetable oil

3 garlic cloves, minced

3 teaspoons minced ginger

6 green onions, cut diagonally

- Place the shrimp, crab meat and scallops in a shallow dish. Combine 1/4 cup sherry, salt and white pepper in a bowl and mix well. Pour over the seafood.
- Combine the soy sauce, white vinegar, 3 tablespoons sherry, chicken broth, brown sugar and cornstarch in a bowl and mix well.
- Heat 6 tablespoons oil in a wok over high heat. Stir-fry the chile peppers and cashews until slightly charred. Remove from the wok.
- Add 4 tablespoons oil to the wok. Add the garlic and ginger and stir-fry. Stir in the green onions and seafood mixture. Cook for 5 minutes. Add the soy sauce mixture, cooked chile peppers and cooked cashews. Cook until the mixture is thickened, stirring frequently.
- *Yield: 8 to 12 servings*

1 (12-ounce) bottle chili sauce
1 tablespoon prepared horseradish
1 tablespoon lemon juice
1/2 teaspoon Worcestershire sauce
1/4 teaspoon salt
Dash of pepper

Combine the chili sauce, horseradish, lemon juice, Worcestershire sauce, salt and pepper in a bowl and mix well. Chill, covered, in the refrigerator. Toss with boiled shrimp for a delicious Shrimp Cocktail.

Savannah Seafood Casserole

8 ounces small seashell pasta
4 cups milk
1/2 cup flour
2 cups shredded sharp cheese
1/2 teaspoon mace
1 teaspoon salt
1 teaspoon dry mustard
1/2 teaspoon white pepper
Dash of Tabasco sauce
3 or more dashes of
 Worcestershire sauce
1 (2-ounce) jar chopped
 pimentos

4 ounces mushrooms, sliced
1/2 cup (1 stick) butter
1/2 cup finely chopped celery
1/2 cup finely chopped green
 bell pepper
1/2 cup finely chopped
 Vidalia onion
1 pound lump or claw crab meat
1 pound cooked shrimp
Bread crumbs
Butter

- Cook the pasta using the package directions; drain.
- Pour the milk into a saucepan. Whisk in the flour gradually. Bring to a boil, stirring constantly. Stir in the cheese. Cook until the cheese is melted, stirring constantly. Place the cheese mixture in a double boiler over simmering water. Add the mace, salt, dry mustard, white pepper, Tabasco sauce, Worcestershire sauce, pimentos and mushrooms and mix well.
- Heat 1/2 cup butter in a skillet until melted. Add the celery, bell pepper and onion. Sauté until tender. Spoon into the cheese mixture. Add the cooked pasta, crab meat and shrimp to the cheese mixture and stir gently.
- Spoon the seafood mixture into a buttered 9×12-inch baking dish. Sprinkle bread crumbs lightly over the seafood mixture. Dot with butter. Bake at 350 degrees until hot and bubbly. You may bake this in two smaller baking dishes or in ramekins.
- *Yield: 8 to 10 servings*

Marinated Grouper with Fruit Salsa

½ cup lime juice

¼ cup tequila

2 tablespoons chopped cilantro

1 medium shallot, chopped

1 garlic clove, chopped

4 grouper fillets

Fruit Salsa

- Combine the lime juice, tequila, cilantro, shallot and garlic in a small bowl and mix well. Let stand at room temperature to enhance the flavors.
- Brush the lime mixture over the grouper fillets 15 to 20 minutes before grilling. Place the grouper fillets on a grill over hot coals. Grill until the grouper flakes easily. Place on individual serving plates. Spoon Fruit Salsa over the top.
- *Yield: 4 servings*

Fruit Salsa

½ fresh pineapple, finely
   chopped

½ cup finely chopped
   strawberries

¼ cup finely chopped kiwifruit

1 medium shallot or green
   onion, chopped

Cilantro to taste

Juice of 1 lime or lemon

Salt to taste

2 tablespoons chopped jalapeño
   pepper

- Combine the pineapple, strawberries, kiwifruit, shallot, cilantro, lime juice, salt and jalapeño pepper in a bowl and mix well.
- You may substitute seasonal fruits for the pineapple, strawberries and kiwifruit.

Flounder Roll-Ups

1 cup stuffing mix
2 tablespoons vegetable
  oil

1 (10-ounce) can cream of
  shrimp soup
4 to 6 flounder fillets

- Combine the stuffing mix, oil, 3 tablespoons of the soup and a dash of water in a bowl and mix well. Spread evenly over the flounder fillets. Roll up each fillet loosely. Place seam side down in a baking dish. Brush a small amount of the soup over the tops.
- Bake at 350 degrees for 40 minutes. Cook the remaining soup in a saucepan until heated through. Spoon over the roll-ups.
- *Yield: 4 to 6 servings*

Salmon Dijon

Dijon mustard for coating
2 skinless salmon fillets
¹⁄₄ cup bread crumbs
2 tablespoons parsley

¹⁄₄ cup finely chopped walnuts
  or pecans
2 tablespoons butter, melted

- Spread the mustard generously over the salmon. Combine the bread crumbs, parsley, walnuts and butter in a shallow dish and mix well. Dredge the salmon in the mixture, coating both sides. Place in a shallow baking dish.
- Bake at 450 degrees for 20 minutes.
- *Yield: 2 to 4 servings*

Desserts

Women in China
Hold Up Half the Sky
Harriet Marshall Goode

Harriet Marshall Goode

Harriet Marshall Goode's painting Women in China
Hold Up Half the Sky *was one of the first in her series
of Chinese women. The title, which is written in
Chinese across the painting, is a motto promoted by
Chairman Mao. She feels that artists are able to resolve
personal dilemmas or to work through times of stress by
allowing emotions to steer the direction, letting the piece
"paint itself."*

*Harriet Marshall Goode, affectionately known by
most as "Sister," was born and raised in Rock Hill. She
has painted since her early college days and has been a
working artist for almost twenty years. Sister's work has
won numerous honors and awards and can be seen in
private and corporate collections throughout the United
States, Europe, China, Canada, and Mexico.*

Applesauce Brûlée

3 pounds Granny Smith apples, peeled, cored
Salt to taste
2 tablespoons butter
2 teaspoons cinnamon
1 teaspoon nutmeg
¹/₂ to 1 cup packed brown sugar
2 cups sour cream
Brown sugar for topping

- Combine the apples with enough water to cover in a large saucepan. Bring to a boil. Cook until soft. Stir in the salt, butter, cinnamon, nutmeg and enough of the ¹/₂ to 1 cup brown sugar to make of the desired sweetness. Remove from the heat. Let stand until cool.
- Process the apple mixture in a blender until smooth. Spoon 4 cups of the applesauce evenly into a soufflé dish. Spread the sour cream evenly over the top. Let stand until room temperature.
- Sift brown sugar over the top. Place under a preheated broiler and broil until caramelized.
- *Yield: 6 to 8 servings*

This 4th of July parade started in 1977 on July 3rd. Johnny Johnson and a group of his high school friends were over at Becky and Ed Thompson's house (next-door neighbors). The teenagers were complaining that there was nothing to do in Rock Hill on the 4th of July. Johnny's daddy said that if they would all come to his house the next day, they could have a parade. Everybody took him up on it! Doug Herlong went to Burns Chevrolet and got a flatbed truck, and Susu Jenkins (Cox) crowned herself the first queen and showed up in the back of Caughman Taylor's convertible. It was just two vehicles that first year and they rode all over town. Of course, the parade was such fun it continues today.

After the parade, everyone brought a dish to share. A favorite was Nelle Givens' Banana Pudding.

Nelle Givens' Banana Pudding

3 (4-ounce) packages vanilla instant pudding mix
5 cups milk
9 ounces whipped topping
1 cup sour cream
8 or 9 bananas, sliced
1 (16-ounce) package vanilla wafers

- Beat the pudding mix and milk in a mixing bowl until smooth. Fold in the whipped topping and sour cream. Layer the pudding mixture, bananas and wafers in a 3-quart dish. Chill, covered, for 1 day for enhanced flavor.
- *Yield: 10 to 12 servings*

Banana Split Brownie Pizza

1 (21-ounce) package brownie mix
16 ounces cream cheese, softened
2/3 cup sugar
1 (8-ounce) can pineapple tidbits
3 bananas, sliced
1 pint strawberries, sliced
1/2 cup chopped pecans, toasted
1 ounce semisweet chocolate
1 tablespoon butter or margarine

- Prepare the brownie mix using the package directions. Spread the batter over the bottom of a greased 15-inch pizza pan. Bake at 375 degrees for 15 to 20 minutes or until brownies pull from the side of the pan. Let stand until cool. Beat the cream cheese and sugar in a mixing bowl until smooth. Spread over the cooled brownie crust. Drain the pineapple and pat dry.
- Arrange the pineapple, bananas, strawberries and pecans over the cream cheese layer. Combine the chocolate and butter in a microwave-safe measuring cup. Microwave on High for 1 minute, stirring after 30 seconds. Drizzle over the fruit. Chill, covered, for 1 hour.
- *Yield: 12 servings*

Chocolate Icebox Cake

Mrs. F. W. Faircloth (Brucie), Past President, 1957–1958

1 (6-ounce) package vanilla cook-and-serve pudding mix
2 teaspoons instant coffee granules
1 envelope unflavored gelatin
1 cup milk
2 (8-ounce) bars German's sweet chocolate, broken into pieces
2 cups whipping cream
Sugar to taste
Vanilla extract to taste
2 (16-ounce) packages ladyfingers
Toasted nuts (optional)

- Combine the pudding mix, coffee granules and gelatin in a saucepan. Stir in the milk. Bring to a boil over medium heat, stirring constantly. Boil until the mixture thickens, stirring constantly. Remove from the heat. Stir the chocolate into the hot mixture. Beat until smooth.

- Beat the whipping cream in a mixing bowl until soft peaks form. Beat in sugar and vanilla. Beat until stiff peaks form. Reserve a small amount of the whipped cream in a small bowl. Chill, covered, in the refrigerator. Fold the remaining whipped cream into the chocolate mixture.

- Split the ladyfingers lengthwise. Layer the ladyfingers and chocolate mixture one-half at a time in a long glass dish. Chill, covered, until firm. Spread the reserved whipped cream over the layers. Sprinkle the toasted nuts over the top.

- *Yield: 6 to 8 servings*

Whether or not your favorite team makes it to the Super Bowl, the day of the game is still a good time to get together for a casual Sunday afternoon with friends. Keep it simple. Use baskets, wooden bowls, and your everyday dishes to serve. Or use paper plates and plastic cups. Anything goes! And for a bit of healthy competition, get a football pool going with gag prizes for the winners.

Artichoke Parmesan Dip

Havarti Cheese Spread

Bean Salad

Venison Chili with Bread Bowls

Cheesy French Bread

Key Lime Pie

Chocolate Mint Freeze

Chocolate Mint Freeze

20 to 24 chocolate sandwich cookies

$\frac{1}{2}$ cup (1 stick) margarine

3 ounces semisweet chocolate

3 eggs

2 cups confectioners' sugar

$\frac{1}{2}$ gallon vanilla ice cream, softened

$\frac{1}{3}$ cup crème de menthe

- Place the chocolate sandwich cookies in a blender container. Process until cookies are fine crumbs. Reserve a small amount of the cookie crumbs. Spread the remaining crumbs over the bottom of a greased 9×13-inch dish.
- Heat the margarine and chocolate in a saucepan over low heat until melted, stirring frequently. Beat the eggs in a small mixing bowl. Stir a small amount of the hot mixture into the beaten eggs. Stir the eggs into the hot mixture. Cook until thickened, stirring constantly. Add the confectioners' sugar and mix well. Pour over the cookie crumbs in the prepared dish. Chill until firm.
- Combine the ice cream and crème de menthe in a bowl and mix well. Spread over the chocolate layer. Sprinkle with the reserved cookie crumbs. Freeze, covered, until frozen through. Cut into bars.
- *Yield: 2 dozen bars*

Chocolate Mousse Parfaits with Raspberry Purée

1/2 cup whipping cream
16 ounces semisweet chocolate
1/2 cup light corn syrup
1/2 cup (1 stick) butter
1 1/2 cups whipping cream
1/4 cup confectioners' sugar, sifted
1 teaspoon vanilla extract
10 ounces raspberries
3 to 4 tablespoons confectioners' sugar (optional)
Fresh mint sprigs or fresh whole raspberries for garnish

- Combine 1/2 cup whipping cream, chocolate, corn syrup and butter in a heavy saucepan. Cook over low heat until the chocolate melts, stirring constantly. Let stand until cool.
- Beat 1 1/2 cups whipping cream, 1/4 cup confectioners' sugar and vanilla in a mixing bowl at high speed until stiff peaks form. Fold into the cooled chocolate mixture. Spoon into 16 parfait glasses. Chill, covered, for 8 hours or longer.
- Process 10 ounces raspberries in a blender container until smooth, scraping down the sides. Strain using a fine wire mesh strainer and discarding the seeds. Combine with enough of the 3 to 4 tablespoons confectioners' sugar to make of the desired sweetness. Chill, covered, in the refrigerator.
- Spoon the raspberry purée over the chocolate mousse. Garnish with mint sprigs or whole raspberries.
- *Yield: 16 servings*

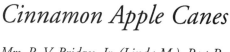

Cinnamon Apple Canes

Mrs. R. V. Bridges, Jr. (Linda M.), Past President, 1986–1987

1 cup milk	1 cup (2 sticks) margarine
1 envelope dry yeast	2 eggs
1/4 cup warm water	2 cups finely chopped apples
4 cups flour	1/3 cup sugar
1/4 cup sugar	3/4 cup finely chopped pecans
1 teaspoon salt	1 1/2 teaspoons cinnamon

- Scald the milk in a saucepan. Cool to lukewarm. Dissolve the yeast in the warm water in a small bowl. Combine the flour, 1/4 cup sugar and salt in a bowl and mix well. Cut in the margarine until crumbly. Add the yeast mixture, lukewarm milk and eggs and mix well. Chill, tightly covered, for 2 to 48 hours.
- Combine the apples, 1/3 cup sugar, pecans and cinnamon in a saucepan. Cook over medium heat until the apples are tender, stirring frequently.
- Preheat oven to 400 degrees. Divide the dough into 2 equal portions. Roll 1 portion into a 15×18-inch rectangle on a lightly floured surface. Spread half the apple mixture down the center. Fold the sides over the center to enclose the filling. Cut into 15 strips. Twist each strip, pinching the ends to seal. Shape into canes on a lightly greased baking sheet. Repeat the process with the remaining dough and remaining apple mixture.
- Bake for 10 to 15 minutes or until golden brown. Cool on a wire rack. You may frost the apple canes with a confectioners' sugar frosting.
- *Yield: 2 1/2 dozen*

Meringue Dessert

Mrs. A. F. Marshall (Harriet), Past (First) President, 1938–1939

8 egg whites
1 teaspoon cream of tartar
2 cups sugar
1 teaspoon vanilla extract
1 teaspoon white vinegar

Lemon Filling
Sweetened whipped cream and
curls of lemon zest or sprigs
of mint for garnish

- Beat the egg whites with the cream of tartar in a mixing bowl until soft peaks form. Add the sugar gradually, beating until stiff peaks form. Beat in the vanilla and vinegar.
- Spoon dollops onto a baking sheet covered with brown paper. Make an indentation in each meringue with the back of a spoon. Bake at 275 degrees for 2 hours. Cool on a wire rack.
- Fill the indentation in each meringue with Lemon Filling. Garnish with sweetened whipped cream and a curl of lemon zest or a sprig of mint.
- *Yield: 1½ dozen*

Lemon Filling

5 egg yolks
Juice of 3 lemons
1 tablespoon butter

1 cup sugar
2 tablespoons cornstarch

- Combine the egg yolks, lemon juice, butter, sugar and cornstarch in a double boiler and mix well. Cook until the mixture is thickened, stirring constantly.

DESSERTS

PAST PRESIDENTS

In many ways my mother's life was like a tapestry— woven of fine and rare threads into strong and beautiful cloth. She actually was an accomplished seamstress and until the mid-1950s made everyday dresses as well as party dresses and ball gowns for my three sisters and me. And it always amazed me that during World War II Mother could knit caps and scarves for the soldiers even in the darkness of the Pix Theater!

Mingled with the activities of wife and mother, she made time for volunteerism in the League, as well as church, civic, and social engagements. (Harriet Moore Marshall was the first president of the Junior Welfare League.) She had many of the same ideas about community service in the 1930s that are still relevant today.

A tribute to Harriet Marshall

—Mrs. Martin Goode (Harriet Marshall)

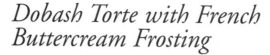

Dobash Torte with French Buttercream Frosting

1 (2-pound) pound cake
1 cup chocolate chips
¼ cup boiling water
⅓ cup confectioners' sugar

4 egg yolks
½ cup (1 stick) butter, softened
1 tablespoon vanilla extract

- Slice the cake horizontally into 7 thin layers. Combine the chocolate chips and boiling water in a blender container. Process on High for 6 seconds or until smooth. Add the confectioners' sugar, egg yolks, butter and vanilla. Process for 15 seconds or until smooth and thick.
- Spread between the layers and over the top and sides of the cake. Chill in the refrigerator. You may freeze the torte. Cut into thin slices.
- *Yield: 10 servings*

Mint Dazzler

¼ cup (½ stick) butter, melted
1¼ cups vanilla wafer crumbs
½ cup (1 stick) butter, softened
½ cup sifted confectioners' sugar
3 eggs, lightly beaten
3 ounces unsweetened chocolate, melted

1 (8-ounce) package miniature marshmallows
1½ cups whipping cream, whipped
½ cup crushed peppermint stick candy

- Combine ¼ cup butter and vanilla wafer crumbs in a bowl and mix well. Press over the bottom of a 9-inch springform pan.
- Cream ½ cup butter and confectioners' sugar in a mixing bowl. Add the eggs and chocolate, beating until light and fluffy. Pour into the prepared pan. Freeze, covered, until frozen through.
- Decorate the top with the marshmallows, whipped cream and peppermint stick candy as desired.
- *Yield: 12 servings*

Neapolitan Cheesecake

1 cup chocolate wafer cookie
  crumbs
3 tablespoons butter, melted
24 ounces cream cheese,
  softened
3/4 cup sugar
3 eggs
1 teaspoon vanilla extract
2 ounces semisweet chocolate,
  melted

2 ounces white baking
  chocolate, melted
1/3 cup mashed sweetened
  strawberries
3 ounces semisweet chocolate
2 tablespoons butter
1 teaspoon shortening
1/2 ounce white baking chocolate
1 teaspoon shortening

EASY DESSERTS

*You can make an easy dessert
by serving wine, liqueur, or
Champagne over melon balls
in compotes and flavoring it
with grated citrus zest.*

- Combine the cookie crumbs and 3 tablespoons butter in a bowl and mix
  well. Press over the bottom of a 9-inch springform pan. Bake at 350
  degrees for 8 minutes. Let stand until cool.
- Beat the cream cheese and sugar in a mixing bowl until smooth. Add
  the eggs 1 at a time, mixing well after each addition. Beat in the vanilla.
  Divide into 3 equal portions. Stir 2 ounces semisweet chocolate into
  1 portion. Stir 2 ounces white baking chocolate into 1 portion. Stir the
  strawberries into the remaining portion. Spread the semisweet chocolate
  mixture over the crust. Spread the white chocolate mixture carefully over
  the semisweet chocolate layer. Spread the strawberry mixture over the white
  chocolate layer.
- Bake at 425 degrees for 10 minutes. Reduce the oven temperature to
  300 degrees. Bake for an additional 50 to 55 minutes or until almost set.
  Loosen the cheesecake from the side of the pan with a knife. Cool on a
  wire rack. Remove from the pan.
- Combine 3 ounces semisweet chocolate, 2 tablespoons butter and
  1 teaspoon shortening in a saucepan. Cook until melted, stirring
  constantly. Pour over the cheesecake. Combine 1/2 ounce white chocolate
  and 1 teaspoon shortening in a saucepan. Cook until melted, stirring
  constantly. Drizzle over the cheesecake. Chill in the refrigerator.
- *Yield: 12 to 14 servings*

Pears Baked in Cream

1 tablespoon butter

1 tablespoon sugar

2 Bosc or Bartlett pears, cut into halves, cored

1 tablespoon sugar

1 tablespoon butter

½ cup heavy cream

- Spread 1 tablespoon butter over the bottom and side of a shallow baking dish. Sprinkle with 1 tablespoon sugar. Arrange the pears cut side down in the prepared dish. Sprinkle with 1 tablespoon sugar. Dot with 1 tablespoon butter. Bake at 400 degrees for 10 minutes.
- Pour the cream over the pears. Bake for an additional 20 minutes. Serve warm.
- *Yield: 4 servings*

Peppermint Parfaits

½ gallon vanilla ice cream, softened

30 red starlight mints, crushed

10 peppermint candy canes for garnish

- Layer the ice cream and mints alternately in 10 parfait or wine glasses until all of the ingredients are used, beginning and ending with the ice cream. Freeze, covered, for up to 2 hours. Garnish with the peppermint candy canes.
- *Yield: 10 servings*

Tiramisu

²/₃ cup sifted confectioners' sugar

8 ounces reduced-fat cream cheese

1 cup whipped topping

¹/₂ cup sugar

¹/₄ cup water

3 egg whites

¹/₂ cup hot water

1 tablespoon sugar

1 tablespoon instant espresso granules

¹/₄ cup Kahlúa or other coffee-flavor liqueur

20 ladyfingers, split, or an equivalent amount of sponge cake

¹/₂ cup whipped topping

¹/₂ teaspoon baking cocoa

- Beat the confectioners' sugar and cream cheese in a mixing bowl at high speed until well blended. Fold in 1 cup whipped topping.
- Combine ¹/₂ cup sugar, ¹/₄ cup water and egg whites in the top of a double boiler. Place over simmering water. Beat with an electric mixer at high speed until stiff peaks form. Fold one-fourth of the beaten egg whites into the cream cheese mixture. Fold the remaining egg white mixture into the cream cheese mixture.
- Combine ¹/₂ cup hot water, 1 tablespoon sugar, espresso granules and Kahlúa in a bowl and mix well.
- Arrange half the ladyfingers cut side up over the bottom of an 8×8-inch baking dish. Drizzle half the espresso mixture over the ladyfingers. Spread half the cream cheese mixture over the ladyfingers. Arrange the remaining ladyfingers over the cream cheese layer. Drizzle with the remaining espresso mixture. Spread the remaining cream cheese mixture over the ladyfingers. Spread ¹/₂ cup whipped topping over the layers. Sprinkle with the baking cocoa.
- *Yield: 4 to 8 servings*

Bananas in Orange Apricot Sauce

Mrs. Craig T. Ferguson (Susan R.), Past President, 1998–1999

4 ounces dried apricots, chopped	**1¹/₂ cups orange juice**
¹/₂ cup water	**¹/₂ cup sugar**
4 teaspoons cornstarch	**4 large bananas, sliced**

• Combine the apricots and water in a saucepan. Bring to a boil. Remove from the heat. Whisk the cornstarch and orange juice in a separate saucepan until smooth. Bring to a boil over medium heat, whisking constantly. Remove from the heat. Stir in the sugar. Add the apricots and mix well. Chill, covered, in the refrigerator. Stir in the bananas. Serve immediately or chill, covered, in the refrigerator for up to 3 days. You may serve this over ice cream or pound cake.

• *Yield: 6 servings*

Spicy Fruit

8 whole cloves	**4 teaspoons instant tapioca**
8 ounces prunes, chopped	**¹/₄ teaspoon salt**
8 ounces dried apricots, chopped	**¹/₂ cup sugar**
¹/₂ teaspoon ground ginger	**1 cup orange juice**
2 cups water	**1 cup chopped walnuts**

• Tie the cloves in cheesecloth or a coffee filter. Combine the cloves, prunes, apricots, ginger, water, tapioca and salt in a saucepan. Bring to a boil. Reduce the heat. Simmer for 1 to 2 minutes. Stir in the sugar and orange juice. Bring to a boil. Stir in the walnuts. Remove the cloves. Serve immediately or chill, covered, in the refrigerator for up to 3 days. You may serve this over ice cream or pound cake.

• *Yield: 8 servings*

Roscoe's Special

½ cup (1 stick) butter
2 ounces unsweetened chocolate
2 cups packed brown sugar or
    confectioners' sugar

1 (5-ounce) can evaporated milk
4 to 6 slices pound cake, toasted
4 to 6 scoops vanilla ice cream

- Combine the butter, chocolate, brown sugar and evaporated milk in a saucepan. Cook until heated through and smooth, stirring constantly.
- Place a slice of pound cake on each dessert plate. Place a scoop of ice cream on the pound cake. Spoon the hot fudge sauce over the top.
- *Yield: 4 to 6 servings*

Cheerwine Ice Cream

2 (14-ounce) cans sweetened
    condensed milk
1 (4-ounce) jar maraschino
    cherries, chopped
½ cup chopped pecans

3 (12-ounce) cans Cheerwine
    soda
2 tablespoons vanilla extract
Milk

- Combine the condensed milk, cherries, pecans, soda and vanilla in a bowl and mix well. Pour into an ice cream freezer container. Add milk to the fill line. Freeze using manufacturer's directions.
- *Yield: Variable*

ROSCOE'S SPECIAL

In Rock Hill during the 1940s to the 1950s, there was a popular soda shop on Myrtle Drive. The Good Shop served sandwiches, ice cream, and sodas. Lots of good times were had by local high school and Winthrop students. Roscoe's Special was one of the most popular menu items and is still a favorite of supper club groups.

Vanilla Soufflé

1 (2-ounce) package slivered
  almonds
1 pint vanilla ice cream, softened
8 to 10 small coconut
  macaroons, finely crushed

4 teaspoons Grand Marnier
2 teaspoons confectioners' sugar
$\frac{1}{2}$ cup whipping cream,
  whipped
Strawberry Sauce

- Spread the almonds over a baking sheet. Bake at 350 degrees for 10 minutes or until toasted. Let stand until cool. Chop the almonds finely.
- Beat the ice cream in a mixing bowl until smooth. Add the macaroons and Grand Marnier and mix well. Set aside a small amount of the almonds. Add the remaining almonds to the ice cream mixture and mix well. Stir the confectioners' sugar into the whipped cream. Fold the sweetened whipped cream into the ice cream mixture. Spoon into a soufflé dish. Sprinkle with the reserved almonds. Freeze, covered, until frozen through.
- Spoon the soufflé onto serving dishes. Serve with the Strawberry Sauce.
- *Yield: 4 servings*

Strawberry Sauce

1 (10-ounce) package frozen
  strawberries, thawed

Sugar to taste
4 teaspoons Grand Marnier

- Cook the strawberries in a saucepan until tender. Stir in enough sugar to make of the desired sweetness. Remove from the heat. Stir in the Grand Marnier. Chill, covered, in the refrigerator.

Foba's Apple Dapple Cake

1½ cups vegetable oil

3 eggs

2 cups sugar

2 teaspoons vanilla extract

3 cups flour, sifted

1 teaspoon salt

1½ teaspoons baking soda

1 teaspoon cinnamon

1 teaspoon nutmeg

1 cup pecans, chopped

3 cups chopped apples

1 cup packed brown sugar

¼ cup milk

½ cup (1 stick) margarine

- Beat the oil, eggs and sugar in a mixing bowl until well blended. Beat in the vanilla. Add the flour, salt, baking soda, cinnamon and nutmeg and mix well. Fold in the pecans and apples. Spoon into a greased tube pan. Bake at 350 degrees for 1 hour. Combine the brown sugar, milk and margarine in a saucepan. Cook over low heat until the mixture is smooth, stirring frequently. Cook for 3 minutes, stirring frequently. Pour the hot glaze over the hot cake. Let stand for 2 hours. Remove from the pan.

- *Yield: 8 to 10 servings*

Bourbon Cake

1 (2-layer) butter-recipe
   cake mix

½ cup (1 stick) butter

1½ cups sugar

3 eggs, beaten

¼ cup bourbon

1 cup chopped pecans

1 cup shredded coconut

Whipped cream or whipped
   topping

Praline or vanilla ice cream

- Prepare and bake the cake mix using the package directions for a 2-layer cake. Remove to a wire rack to cool completely. Cut each layer into halves horizontally. Combine the butter, sugar, eggs and bourbon in a saucepan. Bring to a boil, stirring constantly. Cook until the mixture thickens. Stir in the pecans and coconut. Spread between the layers of the cake. Spread the whipped cream over the top of the cake. Serve with praline ice cream.

- *Yield: 12 servings*

Top off an entertaining evening at Byrnes Auditorium with coffee and desserts for a small group. Set up a coffee bar with flavored liqueurs and toppings and a delectable spread of desserts. Most of these sweets can be made ahead. Simply slip out of Byrnes before the last number or encore, if possible, and start the coffee brewing. Bravo!

Coffee with Flavored Liqueurs
Bourbon Cake
Date Nut Balls
Chocolate Praline Layer Cake
Butternut Pound Cake with
  Fresh Strawberries
Neapolitan Cheesecake

Chocolate Praline Layer Cake

½ cup (1 stick) butter or
  margarine
½ cup heavy cream
1 cup packed brown sugar
¾ cup coarsely chopped pecans
1 (2-layer) package devil's food
  cake mix
1¼ cups water
⅓ cup vegetable oil
3 eggs
Whipped Cream Topping
Whole pecans for garnish
Chocolate curls for garnish

- Preheat oven to 325 degrees. Combine the butter, cream and brown sugar in a saucepan. Cook over low heat until the butter is melted, stirring occasionally. Pour into two 8-inch round cake pans. Sprinkle the pecans evenly over the brown sugar mixture.
- Combine the cake mix, water, oil and eggs in a mixing bowl. Beat at low speed until moistened. Beat at high speed for 2 minutes. Spoon the batter evenly over the pecan mixture.
- Bake for 35 to 45 minutes or until the cake springs back when touched lightly in the center. Cool in the pans for 5 minutes. Remove to a wire rack to cool completely.
- Place 1 layer praline side up on a serving plate. Spread half the Whipped Cream Topping over the layer. Place the remaining layer praline side up over the Whipped Cream Topping. Spread the remaining Whipped Cream Topping over the layer. Garnish with whole pecans and chocolate curls. Chill until ready to serve.
- *Yield: 12 servings*

Whipped Cream Topping

1¾ cups whipping cream
¼ cup confectioners' sugar
¼ teaspoon vanilla extract

- Beat the whipping cream in a mixing bowl until soft peaks form. Add the confectioners' sugar and vanilla. Beat until stiff peaks form.

Chocolate Roll

Mrs. Phillip C. Okey (Suzanne), Past President, 1984–1985

5 egg whites	**2 cups whipping cream**
5 egg yolks	**1/2 cup (scant) sugar**
1/2 cup sugar	**1/2 teaspoon vanilla extract**
2 tablespoons baking cocoa	**Chocolate Sauce**
Pinch of salt	

- Preheat oven to 400 degrees. Beat the egg whites in a mixing bowl until stiff peaks form. Beat the egg yolks in a separate mixing bowl until thick and pale yellow. Add 1/2 cup sugar, baking cocoa and salt and mix well. Fold in the egg whites. Spread the batter evenly in a buttered and floured 12×15-inch cake pan. Bake for 15 minutes. Invert the cake onto a damp cloth. Cover with another damp cloth.
- Beat the whipping cream, scant 1/2 cup sugar and vanilla in a mixing bowl until stiff peaks form. Remove the cover cloth. Spread the whipped cream mixture over the cake. Roll the cake as for a jelly roll from the short side. Place seam side down on a serving plate. Spread with the Chocolate Sauce or serve the Chocolate Sauce with cake slices. You may freeze the Chocolate Roll.
- *Yield: 4 servings*

Chocolate Sauce

6 ounces bittersweet chocolate, broken	**2 tablespoons butter**
	1/2 cup heavy cream

- Heat the chocolate in the top of a double boiler over hot but not boiling water until melted. Add the butter. Cook, stirring until smooth. Stir in the cream.

*Summer afternoon—
Summer afternoon; to me
those have always been the
two most beautiful words in
the English language.*

—Henry James

Harvey Wallbanger Cake

Mrs. J. D. Pilcher (Natalie S.), Past President, 1949–1950

1 (2-layer) package lemon cake mix	1/4 cup vodka
1 (4-ounce) package lemon instant pudding mix	1/4 cup galliano
1/2 cup vegetable oil	1/2 cup frozen orange juice concentrate, thawed
1/2 cup sugar	1/4 cup water
4 eggs	3/4 cup confectioners' sugar
	Orange juice

- Mix the first 9 ingredients in a mixing bowl. Beat for 4 minutes or until smooth and creamy. Pour into a greased bundt pan. Bake at 350 degrees for 45 minutes. Cool in the pan for 10 minutes. Invert onto a serving plate.
- Combine the confectioners' sugar and enough orange juice to make of the desired consistency in a bowl and mix well. Pour over the cake.
- *Yield: 16 servings*

Butternut Pound Cake

3 cups flour	3 cups sugar
1/2 teaspoon baking powder	6 eggs
1/2 teaspoon salt	1 cup milk
1 cup (2 sticks) butter, softened	1 tablespoon butternut flavoring
1/2 cup shortening	Fresh strawberries for garnish

- Sift the flour, baking powder and salt together. Cream the butter, shortening and sugar in a mixing bowl until light and fluffy. Beat in the eggs 1 at a time. Add the sifted dry ingredients alternately with the milk, mixing well after each addition. Stir in the butternut flavoring. Pour into a greased tube pan. Place in a cold oven. Bake at 325 degrees for 1 1/2 hours or until the cake begins to pull from the side of the pan. Cool in the pan for 10 minutes. Remove to a wire rack to cool completely. Garnish with fresh strawberries.
- *Yield: 16 servings*

Half-Pound Cake

Mrs. Rea K. Cauthen (Frances Sullivan), Past President, 1966–1967

1 cup (2 sticks) butter, softened	**2 cups flour**
1²/₃ cups sugar	**¹/₂ teaspoon salt**
5 eggs	**2 teaspoons vanilla extract**

- Cream the butter and sugar in a mixing bowl until light and fluffy. Add the eggs 1 at a time, mixing well after each addition. Add the flour, salt and vanilla and mix well. Pour into a greased tube pan. Place in a cold oven. Bake at 325 degrees for 50 to 55 minutes or until a wooden pick inserted in the center comes out clean. Cool in the pan for 10 minutes. Remove to a wire rack to cool completely.
- *Yield: 16 servings*

Sour Cream Pound Cake

3 cups flour	**1 cup (2 sticks) butter, softened**
¹/₄ teaspoon baking soda	**6 egg yolks**
6 egg whites	**1 cup sour cream**
3 cups sugar	

- Sift the flour and baking soda together. Beat the egg whites in a mixing bowl until stiff peaks form.
- Cream the sugar and butter in a mixing bowl until light and fluffy. Add the egg yolks 1 at a time, mixing well after each addition. Add the sifted dry ingredients alternately with the sour cream, blending well after each addition. Fold in the beaten egg whites.
- Pour into a greased 10-inch tube pan. Bake at 325 degrees for 1 to 1¹/₂ hours or until the cake is light brown on top and begins to pull from the side of the pan. Cool in the pan.
- *Yield: 16 servings*

As a child, I can remember my mother baking her Red Velvet Cake. Word got out in the community about how good the cake was, and one day the Evening Herald *(local paper) came to our house to photograph her baking it. This cake became the centerpiece of my mother's annual Valentine's party.*

—Daphne Sutton Mahon

The Original Red Velvet Cake

¼ cup red food coloring	1 cup buttermilk
1 tablespoon baking cocoa	1 teaspoon salt
½ cup shortening	1 teaspoon vanilla extract
1½ cups sugar	1 teaspoon vinegar
2 eggs	1 teaspoon baking soda
2¼ cups flour	Red Velvet Frosting

- Preheat oven to 350 degrees. Combine the food coloring and baking cocoa in a bowl and mix well. Cream the shortening and sugar in a mixing bowl until light and fluffy. Add the eggs 1 at a time, mixing well after each addition. Add the food coloring mixture and mix well. Add the flour, buttermilk, salt and vanilla and mix well. Fold in the vinegar and baking soda. Pour into three 8-inch round cake pans. Bake for 35 minutes.
- Cool in the pans for 10 minutes. Remove to a wire rack to cool completely. Spread the Red Velvet Frosting between the layers and over the top and side of the cooled cake.
- *Yield: 16 servings*

Red Velvet Frosting

3 tablespoons cornstarch	1½ cups (3 sticks) butter,
1½ cups water	softened
1½ cups sugar	1½ teaspoons vanilla extract

- Combine the cornstarch and water in a saucepan, whisking until smooth. Cook until thick, stirring frequently. Let stand until cool.
- Cream the sugar, butter and vanilla in a mixing bowl until light and fluffy. Add the cornstarch mixture and mix well. Beat until the consistency of whipped cream.

Sherry Cake

Mrs. Melvin Cauthen (Joanne Emerson), Past President, 1965–1966

1 angel food cake
1 envelope unflavored gelatin
¼ cup cold water
4 egg yolks
½ cup sugar
½ cup sherry or cooking sherry
4 egg whites
½ cup sugar
2 cups whipping cream
1 teaspoon vanilla extract
1 teaspoon sugar

- Tear the cake into pieces. Arrange the pieces over the bottom of a 4-quart dish.
- Soften the gelatin in the cold water. Combine the egg yolks, ½ cup sugar and sherry in the top of a double boiler and mix well. Cook until the mixture thickens, stirring frequently. Stir in the softened gelatin. Beat the egg whites with ½ cup sugar in a mixing bowl until stiff peaks form. Beat 1 cup of the whipping cream in a separate mixing bowl until stiff peaks form. Fold into the beaten egg whites. Fold in the egg yolk mixture. Pour over the cake. Chill, covered, for 8 to 12 hours.
- Beat the remaining 1 cup whipping cream, vanilla and 1 teaspoon sugar in a mixing bowl until stiff peaks form. Spread over the top of the cake. You may prepare the cake in a bundt pan, invert onto a serving plate and frost with the whipped cream mixture.
- *Yield: 16 servings*

PAST PRESIDENTS

There were a few good eating places in Rock Hill in the 1950s and '60s. Perhaps the best was the dining room in the Andrew Jackson Hotel, now the Guardian Fidelity Building. Our spring luncheons were always held in the ballroom at the Andrew Jackson.

A special treat was to have lunch at the lovely Joe Roddey home on Oakland Avenue, which was across the street from the old Pix Theater. Mrs. Dunlap Roddey, a daughter-in-law, would cater luncheons for book clubs or bridal luncheons and they were always quite a treat.

—Mrs. Melvin Cauthen
(Joanne Emerson)

Turtle Cake

Mrs. Thomas McKinney (Camille Hopkins), Past President, 1977–1978

**1 (2-layer) package German chocolate
cake mix**
1 (14-ounce) package caramels
½ cup evaporated milk
¾ cup (1½ sticks) butter, melted
1 cup pecans
1 cup chocolate chips
1 cup pecans

- Prepare the cake mix using the package directions. Pour half the batter
  into a greased 9×13-inch cake pan. Bake at 350 degrees for 15 minutes.
- Combine the caramels, evaporated milk and butter in a medium heavy
  saucepan. Cook over low heat until the caramels are melted, stirring
  constantly. Pour over the cake.
- Sprinkle 1 cup pecans and chocolate chips over the top of the caramel layer.
  Pour the remaining batter over the pecans and chocolate chips. Sprinkle
  with 1 cup pecans. Bake for an additional 20 minutes.
- *Yield: 15 servings*

White Wine Cake

¹/₂ cup chopped pecans

1 (2-layer) package yellow cake mix

1 (4-ounce) package vanilla instant pudding mix

¹/₂ cup water

³/₄ cup vegetable oil

¹/₂ cup white wine

4 eggs

¹/₄ cup sugar

2 teaspoons cinnamon

White Wine Glaze, hot

- Grease and flour a bundt pan. Sprinkle the pecans over the bottom. Combine the cake mix, pudding mix, water, oil, wine, eggs, sugar and cinnamon in a mixing bowl. Beat for 4 minutes or until smooth and creamy. Pour into the prepared pan.
- Bake at 325 degrees for 1 hour. Pour the hot White Wine Glaze over the hot cake. Let stand for 20 minutes or longer. Invert onto a serving plate.
- *Yield: 16 servings*

White Wine Glaze

¹/₂ cup (1 stick) butter

1 cup sugar

¹/₄ cup water

¹/₄ cup white wine

- Combine the butter, sugar and water in a saucepan. Bring to a boil, stirring constantly. Remove from the heat. Stir in the wine.

Grated Apple Pie

1 unbaked (9-inch) pie shell
2 cups grated apples
¼ cup (½ stick) margarine, melted
1 cup sugar
1 egg
1 teaspoon (or more) lemon juice

- Prick the pie shell all over with a fork. Combine the apples, margarine, sugar, egg and lemon juice in a bowl and mix well. Spoon into the pie shell. Bake at 350 degrees for 35 to 40 minutes.
- *Yield: 6 servings*

Caramel Pies

Mrs. Jennings Neely, Sr. (Harriet Dalton), Past President, 1955–1956

1 cup sugar
1½ cups packed brown sugar
¼ cup flour
1 cup (2 sticks) butter, melted
2 tablespoons milk
4 eggs, beaten
1 teaspoon vanilla extract
2 unbaked (9-inch) pie shells

- Combine the sugar, brown sugar, flour, butter, milk, eggs and vanilla in a bowl and mix well. Pour into the pie shells. Bake at 350 degrees for 30 to 40 minutes or until set.
- *Yield: 12 servings*

Chocolate Pie

Mrs. N. F. Yorke (Lane Knox), Past President, 1959–1960

1 cup sugar
2 teaspoons (heaping) baking
  cocoa
2 teaspoons flour
1 cup milk
3 egg yolks, beaten

3/4 cup (1 1/2 sticks) margarine or
  butter, softened
1 teaspoon vanilla extract
1 unbaked (9-inch) pie shell
3 egg whites
1 tablespoon sugar

- Combine 1 cup sugar, baking cocoa and flour in a bowl and mix well. Add the milk, egg yolks, margarine and vanilla and mix until smooth. Pour into the pie shell. Bake at 325 degrees for 30 to 35 minutes or until set.
- Beat the egg whites in a mixing bowl until soft peaks form. Add the sugar, beating until stiff peaks form. Spread over the pie, sealing to the edge. Bake until golden brown.
- *Yield: 6 servings*

Chocolate Oatmeal Pie

2 eggs
1 cup sugar
1/4 teaspoon salt
1 cup light corn syrup
2 tablespoons butter, melted

1 teaspoon vanilla extract
1/2 cup flaked coconut
1/2 cup quick-cooking oats
1/2 cup semisweet chocolate chips
1 unbaked (9-inch) pie shell

- Beat the eggs in a bowl for 5 minutes or until thick and pale yellow. Beat in the sugar, salt, corn syrup, butter and vanilla. Stir in the coconut, oats and chocolate chips. Spoon into the pie shell. Bake at 350 degrees for 40 to 50 minutes or until brown. Cool on a wire rack. Chill, covered, in the refrigerator.
- *Yield: 8 servings*

Key Lime Pie

8 ounces fat-free cream cheese, softened

1 (14-ounce) can fat-free sweetened condensed milk

1 teaspoon vanilla extract

1/3 cup Key lime juice

1 (9-inch) low-fat graham cracker pie shell

- Beat the cream cheese in a mixing bowl until smooth. Beat in the condensed milk gradually. Beat in the vanilla and lime juice. Pour into the pie shell. Chill, covered, for 1 hour or longer.
- *Yield: 8 servings*

Peanut Butter Cream Pie

3/4 cup sugar

1/3 cup flour

1/4 teaspoon salt

2 cups warm milk

3 egg yolks, beaten

1/4 cup (1/2 stick) butter, softened

1 teaspoon vanilla extract

1/2 cup peanut butter

1 baked (9-inch) pie shell

Whipped cream

- Combine the sugar, flour and salt in a saucepan and mix well. Stir in the milk and egg yolks. Cook over medium heat until thickened, stirring constantly. Add the butter and vanilla. Beat until smooth. Let stand until cool. Beat in the peanut butter. Pour into the pie shell. Spread whipped cream over the top. Chill, covered, for 24 hours or freeze for 1 hour.
- *Yield: 6 servings*

Grandmother's Pineapple Coconut Pie

1/2 cup (1 stick) margarine,
   softened
2 cups sugar
4 eggs
1 (8-ounce) can crushed
   pineapple, drained

1 cup packed shredded coconut
1 unbaked (10-inch) deep-dish
   pie shell, or 2 unbaked
   (9-inch) pie shells

- Cream the margarine and sugar in a mixing bowl until light and fluffy.
  Add the eggs 1 at a time, mixing well after each addition. Fold in the
  pineapple and coconut. Spoon into the pie shell. Bake at 350 degrees for
  40 to 45 minutes or until set.
- *Yield: 6 servings*

Vanilla Chip Fruit Tart

3/4 cup (1 1/2 sticks) butter,
   softened
1/2 cup confectioners' sugar
1 1/2 cups flour
1 (10-ounce) package vanilla
   milk chocolate chips

1/4 cup heavy cream
8 ounces cream cheese, softened
Fresh fruits of choice,
   cut into pieces
Apricot preserves

- Cream the butter and confectioners' sugar in a mixing bowl until light and
  fluffy. Add the flour and mix well. Press over the bottom and up the side of
  a 12-inch round baking pan. Bake at 300 degrees for 20 to 25 minutes or
  until golden brown. Let stand until completely cool.
- Place the chocolate chips in a microwave-safe bowl. Microwave for
  1 1/2 minutes. Add the cream and cream cheese, mixing until smooth.
  Spread over the crust. Arrange fruit pieces over the filling. Place preserves
  in a microwave-safe bowl. Microwave until thin. Spread over the fruit.
- *Yield: 10 to 12 servings*

Brown Sugar Pecan Crisps

$1/2$ **cup packed brown sugar**
2 tablespoons margarine or butter, melted
$1/3$ **cup chopped pecans**
$1/2$ **(17-ounce) package frozen puff pastry sheets, thawed**
Confectioners' sugar

- Combine the brown sugar, margarine and pecans in a bowl and mix well. Unfold the pastry on a lightly floured surface. Roll into a 12×15-inch rectangle. Cut into twenty 3-inch squares. Press each square into a 3-inch muffin cup. Place a heaping teaspoon of the pecan mixture over the pastry. Bake at 400 degrees for 12 minutes or until golden brown. Remove from the pan. Cool on a wire rack. Sprinkle with confectioners' sugar.
- *Yield: 20 crisps*

Luscious Lemon Drops

**1 (2-layer) package lemon
  cake mix**
4 ounces whipped topping
1 egg, beaten

1$1/2$ teaspoons lemon juice
1 teaspoon grated lemon zest
Confectioners' sugar for coating

- Combine the cake mix, whipped topping, egg, lemon juice and lemon zest in a bowl and mix well. Shape into small balls. Roll in the confectioners' sugar. Place on a cookie sheet. Bake at 350 degrees for 10 to 12 minutes or until firm. Remove to a wire rack immediately. Let stand until cool.
- *Yield: 4 dozen*

Macadamia Nut Chocolate Chip Cookies

2/3 cup butter or margarine,
   softened
2/3 cup sugar
1/2 cup packed dark brown sugar
1 egg
1 teaspoon vanilla extract

1 1/2 cups flour
9 ounces Swiss dark chocolate,
   cut into 1/2-inch pieces
1 1/2 cups flaked coconut
1 (3-ounce) jar macadamia nuts,
   coarsely chopped

- Cream the butter, sugar and brown sugar in a mixing bowl until light and fluffy. Add the egg and vanilla and mix well. Beat in the flour at low speed until blended. Stir in the chocolate, coconut and nuts.
- Drop by heaping tablespoonfuls 2 1/2 inches apart on a greased cookie sheet. Bake at 325 degrees for 17 minutes or until the edges are light brown and tops look dry. Cool on the cookie sheet for 5 minutes. Remove to a wire rack to cool completely.
- *Yield: 3 dozen*

Molasses Sugar Cookies

2 teaspoons baking soda
2 cups sifted flour
1/2 teaspoon cloves
1/2 teaspoon ginger
1 teaspoon cinnamon
1/2 teaspoon salt

3/4 cup corn oil
1 cup sugar
1/4 cup molasses
1 egg
Sugar for coating

- Sift the baking soda, flour, cloves, ginger, cinnamon and salt together. Combine the corn oil, 1 cup sugar, molasses and egg in a bowl and mix well. Add the sifted dry ingredients and mix well. Chill for 30 minutes. Shape into 1-inch balls. Roll in sugar to coat. Place 2 inches apart on an ungreased cookie sheet. Bake at 375 degrees for 8 to 10 minutes or until firm.
- *Yield: 6 dozen*

World's Best Cookies

2 cups flour
1 teaspoon baking soda
$^1/_2$ teaspoon salt
1 teaspoon baking powder
1 cup sugar
1 cup packed brown sugar
1 cup (2 sticks) butter or margarine, softened
$1^1/_2$ teaspoons vanilla extract
2 eggs
2 cups rolled oats
1 cup chocolate chips
1 cup peanut butter chips
2 cups pecans, chopped

- Sift the flour, baking soda, salt and baking powder together. Cream the sugar, brown sugar and butter in a mixing bowl until light and fluffy. Add the vanilla and eggs and mix well. Beat in the sifted dry ingredients. Stir in the oats, chocolate chips, peanut butter chips and pecans.
- Drop by rounded teaspoonfuls onto an ungreased cookie sheet. Bake at 350 degrees for 10 minutes.
- *Yield: 5 dozen*

Apricot Bars

1 cup flour
1/4 cup sugar
1/2 cup (1 stick) butter
2/3 cup dried apricots
1 cup packed brown sugar
2 eggs

1/3 cup flour
1/2 teaspoon baking powder
1/4 teaspoon salt
1/2 teaspoon vanilla extract
1/2 cup chopped almonds

- Mix 1 cup flour and sugar in a bowl. Cut in the butter until crumbly. Press over the bottom of a 9×9-inch baking pan. Bake at 350 degrees for 20 minutes. Combine the apricots with enough water to cover in a saucepan. Bring to a simmer. Simmer for 10 minutes. Drain and chop the apricots.
- Mix the brown sugar, eggs, 1/3 cup flour, baking powder, salt and vanilla in a bowl. Stir in the apricots and almonds. Spoon evenly over the crust. Bake for 20 to 30 minutes or until light brown. Let cool. Cut into bars.
- *Yield: 3 dozen bars*

Chocolate Chip Brownies

4 ounces unsweetened chocolate
1 cup (2 sticks) butter or
    margarine
2 cups sugar
1 cup flour

4 eggs, beaten
2 teaspoons coffee liqueur,
    brandy or vanilla extract
1 cup semisweet chocolate chips
1 cup chopped nuts

- Combine the chocolate and butter in a heavy 1-quart saucepan. Heat until melted, stirring constantly. Remove from the heat. Mix the sugar and flour in a large bowl. Add the chocolate mixture, eggs and coffee liqueur and mix well. Stir in the chocolate chips and nuts. Spoon into a greased 9×13-inch baking pan. Bake at 325 degrees for 35 minutes or until the brownies pull from the sides of the pan; center will be soft. Cool on a wire rack for 30 to 60 minutes. Cut into squares. Chill for 2 hours or longer.
- *Yield: 4 dozen squares*

NEW YEAR'S EVE PARTY

Many people are choosing to stay home on New Year's Eve and celebrate with friends and family. Do a children's table in the kitchen and include sandwiches, chips, and soft drinks or sparkling cider. Place the adults' food on the dining room table and decorate with anything that sparkles and shines. The hot soup is sure to warm guests after they watch fireworks. And don't forget the bubbly.

Mushroom and Sour Cream Dip

Parmesan-Coated Brie

Hot Crawfish Dip

Herb-Crusted Pork Tenderloins with
    Horseradish Roasted New Potatoes

Antipasto Salad

Black and White Soup

Apricot Bars

Vanilla Soufflé

Bourbon Brownies

1 (21-ounce) package brownie
  mix
1 cup chopped pecans
1/3 cup bourbon
1/2 cup (1 stick) margarine,
  softened

1 to 1 1/2 teaspoons almond
  extract
2 cups confectioners' sugar
2 cups chocolate chips
1 tablespoon shortening

- Prepare and bake the brownie mix using the package directions for a
  9×13-inch baking pan and adding the pecans. Pour the bourbon over the
  hot brownies. Chill, covered, in the refrigerator.
- Beat the margarine, almond extract and confectioners' sugar in a bowl until
  smooth. Spread over the cold brownies. Chill, covered, in the refrigerator.
- Combine the chocolate chips and shortening in a microwave-safe bowl.
  Microwave until melted and mix well. Spread over the layers. Chill,
  covered, in the refrigerator. Cut into bars.
- *Yield: 4 dozen bars*

Butterscotch Bars

2 cups flour
2 teaspoons baking powder
1/2 teaspoon salt
1/2 cup (1 stick) butter
1 (1-pound) package brown
  sugar

2 eggs
1 teaspoon vanilla extract
2 cups chopped black walnuts

- Sift the flour, baking powder and salt together. Melt the butter in a large
  saucepan. Stir in the brown sugar. Add the eggs 1 at a time, mixing well
  after each addition. Add the sifted dry ingredients and mix well. Stir in the
  vanilla. Fold in the walnuts. Spoon into a 9×13-inch baking pan. Bake at
  325 degrees for 25 minutes or until light brown. Cut into bars.
- *Yield: 2 dozen bars*

Charleston Squares

Mrs. Christopher Marion Hicklin (Cathy Rose Beaty),
Past President, 1993–1994

2 cups flour
1 teaspoon baking powder
1/2 teaspoon salt
1/2 cup (1 stick) butter, softened
1 cup sugar
3 egg yolks
2 egg whites
1 teaspoon almond extract
1 teaspoon vanilla extract
1 egg white
1/2 cup packed brown sugar
1/4 teaspoon vanilla extract
1/2 cup chopped nuts
1 (4-ounce) bottle maraschino cherries, finely chopped

- Sift the flour, baking powder and salt together. Cream the butter and sugar in a mixing bowl until light and fluffy. Beat in the egg yolks and 2 egg whites. Add the sifted dry ingredients and mix well. Stir in the almond extract and 1 teaspoon vanilla. Spread over the bottom of a 9×13-inch baking pan.
- Beat 1 egg white until stiff peaks form. Beat in the brown sugar and 1/4 teaspoon vanilla. Spread over the batter. Sprinkle the nuts and cherries over the top. Bake at 350 degrees for 30 minutes; do not overcook. Cut into squares.
- *Yield: 20 squares*

PAST PRESIDENTS

Charleston Squares is a recipe of my Grandmother MacFaddin's. She lived with us and was a great cook and taught me so much about so many things. I can remember as a child cutting the cherries and chopping the nuts for her. She was so patient. She would give Charleston Squares to people at Christmastime or serve them to her church circle or garden or music club. They always looked so pretty and were so moist.

—Mrs. Christopher Marion Hicklin
(Cathy Rose Beaty)

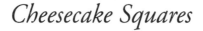

Cheesecake Squares

Mrs. Roy E. Watkins III (Kathy H.), Past President, 1996–1997

2 (8-count) packages crescent rolls
16 ounces cream cheese
1 cup sugar
1 egg
1 teaspoon vanilla extract
¹/₂ cup sugar or packed brown sugar
1 teaspoon cinnamon
¹/₂ cup (1 stick) butter, melted
1 cup chopped pecans

- Unroll the dough in 1 of the packages of crescent rolls. Arrange over the bottom of a greased 9×13-inch baking pan, pressing the perforations to seal. Combine the cream cheese, 1 cup sugar, egg and vanilla in a bowl and beat until smooth. Spread over the dough. Unroll the dough in the remaining package of crescent rolls. Arrange over the cream cheese layer, pressing the perforations to seal.
- Combine ¹/₂ cup sugar, cinnamon, butter and pecans in a bowl and mix well. Pour over the layers. Bake at 350 degrees for 30 minutes. Cut into squares.
- *Yield: 4 dozen squares*

A Great Fudge Bar

1 cup (2 sticks) butter or
   margarine, softened
2 ounces unsweetened chocolate
1½ cups sugar
1 cup flour
¾ to 1¼ cups chopped nuts
1 teaspoon baking powder
2½ teaspoons vanilla extract
3 eggs

8 ounces cream cheese, softened
2 tablespoons flour
1 cup semisweet chocolate chips
   (optional)
2 cups miniature marshmallows
¼ cup milk
1 (1-pound) package
   confectioners' sugar

- Heat ½ cup of the butter and 1 ounce of the chocolate in a large saucepan over low heat until melted, stirring frequently. Remove from the heat. Add 1 cup of the sugar, 1 cup flour, ½ to 1 cup of the nuts, baking powder and 1 teaspoon of the vanilla and mix well. Add 2 of the eggs and mix well. Spread over the bottom of a greased and floured 9×13-inch baking pan.

- Combine 6 ounces of the cream cheese, the remaining ½ cup sugar, 2 tablespoons flour, ¼ cup of the remaining butter, the remaining egg and ½ teaspoon of the remaining vanilla in a mixing bowl and beat until smooth and fluffy. Stir in ¼ cup nuts. Spread over the batter. Sprinkle with the chocolate chips.

- Bake at 350 degrees for 25 to 35 minutes or until a wooden pick inserted in the center comes out clean. Sprinkle with the marshmallows. Bake for an additional 2 minutes.

- Heat the remaining ¼ cup butter, 1 ounce chocolate, 2 ounces cream cheese and milk in a saucepan over low heat until smooth, stirring frequently. Add the confectioners' sugar and remaining 1 teaspoon vanilla and mix until smooth. Pour over the marshmallows and swirl together. Let stand until cool. Cut into bars.

- *Yield: 4 dozen bars*

Lemon Bars

1 cup (2 sticks) butter, softened	6 tablespoons lemon juice
2 cups flour	1 tablespoon (heaping) flour
1/2 cup confectioners' sugar	1/2 teaspoon baking powder
4 eggs	Confectioners' sugar
2 cups sugar	

- Combine the butter, 2 cups flour and 1/2 cup confectioners' sugar in a bowl and mix until smooth. Press over the bottom of a 9×13-inch baking dish. Bake at 325 degrees for 15 minutes.
- Beat the eggs in a bowl with a fork. Add the sugar, lemon juice, 1 tablespoon flour and baking powder and mix well. Pour over the crust. Bake for 40 to 45 minutes or until set. Sprinkle with confectioners' sugar. Let stand for 24 hours. Cut into 2-inch bars. Do not substitute for the butter in this recipe.
- *Yield: 5 dozen bars*

Shortbread

2 cups (4 sticks) butter, softened	1 egg, beaten
1 1/3 cups sugar	4 1/2 cups flour, sifted

- Cream the butter and sugar in a mixing bowl until light and fluffy. Add the egg and mix well. Add the flour and mix well. Press 1/2 inch thick over the bottom of a baking pan. Bake at 275 degrees for 30 to 45 minutes or until golden brown. Let stand until cool. Cut into 2-inch pieces. You may cut with cookie cutters of desired shape and bake on a cookie sheet.
- *Yield: 1 dozen pieces*

Chocolate Scotcheroos

1 cup sugar
1 cup light corn syrup
1 cup peanut butter

6 cups crisp rice cereal
1 cup chocolate chips
1 cup butterscotch chips

- Combine the sugar and corn syrup in a saucepan and mix well. Bring to a boil over medium heat, stirring frequently. Remove from the heat. Add the peanut butter and mix well. Add the crisp rice cereal and mix well. Press the warm mixture evenly over the bottom of a 9×13-inch pan, using a rolling pin to make smooth. Let stand until cool.
- Combine the chocolate chips and butterscotch chips in the top of a double boiler. Cook over hot but not boiling water until melted, stirring constantly. Spread over the rice cereal mixture. Let stand until cool. Cut into bars.
- *Yield: 2 dozen bars*

Date Nut Balls

1 (8-ounce) package sugar dates
½ cup (1 stick) butter
1 cup sugar
1 egg

1 cup pecans
3 cups crisp rice cereal
Confectioners' sugar or coconut
    for coating

- Combine the dates, butter, sugar and egg in a saucepan. Bring to a boil over medium heat, stirring constantly. Boil for 10 minutes, stirring frequently. Let stand until cool. Stir in the pecans and crisp rice cereal.
- Shape into balls. Roll the balls in confectioners' sugar. Store, covered, in the refrigerator.
- *Yield: 4 dozen*

DESERTS

CHRISTMAS COOKIE EXCHANGE

Bring three dozen of your favorite cookies and take home two dozen. The fun comes in choosing from the delicious assortment brought by other guests. Have some snack foods to balance the sweets, and give your friends a wonderful break from the Christmas action.

Pinecone Cheese Ball
Shrimp Paste Finger Sandwiches
Spinach and Cheese Torte
Butterscotch Bars
Molasses Sugar Cookies
Brown Sugar Pecan Crisps
Chocolate Scotcheroos

CONTRIBUTORS

The *Tapestry* Cookbook Committee and the Junior Welfare League of Rock Hill, South Carolina, express appreciation to League members, family, and friends who contributed over seven hundred recipes to *Tapestry*, a weaving of food, culture, and tradition. We deeply regret that we were unable to include all of the wonderful recipes that were submitted, due to availability of space. We hope we have not inadvertently excluded anyone from this list.

Mrs. Barry S. Adickes (Jeannie)
Mrs. Duncan E. Alford (Janet)
Mrs. L. Loyd Ardrey (Barbara)**
Mrs. Gregory S. Ayers (Gidget)
Mrs. Michael R. Baker (Erin)
Mrs. Bryant G. Barnes (Lynn)
Mrs. James L. Barnes (Sherry)
Mrs. John M. Barnes (Jean)**
Mrs. John M. Barnes, Jr. (Martha)
Mrs. R. E. Barron, Jr. (Gladys)
Mrs. W. A. Barron (Bess)**
Mrs. C. Hugh Bates (Daphne)
Mrs. William W. Beaver (Sherrie)
Mrs. Troy A. Began (Michelle)
Mrs. Rod C. Benfield (Melissa)
Mrs. Jeff Blank (Elizabeth)
Mrs. Charles J. Bowers (Susan)
Mrs. R. V. Bridges, Jr. (Linda)**
Mrs. Edward A. Brock (Kim)
Mrs. Wilmot C. Burch (Ann)
Mrs. Charles B. Burnette III (Marcia)**
Mrs. James C. Burnette (Melanie)
Mrs. C. Weldon Burns, Jr. (Rebecca)**
Mrs. Brian P. Carter (Nancy)
Mrs. David D. Casey (Ann)
Mrs. Joseph C. Cauthen IV (Carolyn)
Mrs. Melvin B. Cauthen (Joanne)**
Mrs. Rea K. Cauthen (Frances)**
Mrs. Barry Chitwood (Cynthia)
Mrs. Dennis M. Clemens (Mary)
Mrs. Michael W. Climer (Kim)
Mrs. H. Leon Comer, Jr. (Judy)
Mrs. Stephen J. Cooley (Cindy)
Mrs. Paul S. Coombs, Jr. (Karen)

Mrs. Timothy F. Cooper (Libby)
Mrs. William C. Corn (Pam)
Mrs. Coy F. Coulson (Jodie)
Mrs. Michael S. Crippen (Elizabeth)
Mrs. William L. Culp, Jr. (Janice)
Mrs. Cameron S. Davidson (Amy)
Mrs. Rutledge H. DePass (Peggy)
Mrs. Harry A. Dest (Quida)
Mrs. Hugh B. Dickey III (Cindy)
Mrs. Jefferson R. Dill (Laura)
Mrs. Paul W. Dillingham (Paula)
Mrs. Eugene Dixon (Dorothy)
Mrs. Larry C. Doggett (Susie)
Mrs. Rick Dove (Susan)
Mrs. Phillip E. Dressler (Julie)
Mrs. Frank B. Eaves, Jr. (Susan)
Mrs. Doug Echols (Sylvia)
Mrs. Forrest M. Emerson (Linda)
Mrs. Fred W. Faircloth, Jr. (Brucie)**
Mrs. Fredrick W. Faircloth III (Phyllis)**
Mrs. Craig T. Ferguson (Susan)**
Mrs. Don P. Ferguson (Phyllis)**
Mrs. Samuel B. Fewell, Jr. (Kerrina)
Mrs. Robert V. Fulmer (Mary Anna)
Mrs. David M. Gault (Beth)
Mrs. James P. Gill (Cathy)
Mrs. Thomas A. Givens (Donna)
Mrs. William P. Gladden, Jr. (Kim)
Mrs. John D. Good III (Vivienne)**
Mrs. John D. Good IV (Wendy)
Mrs. Martin Goode (Harriet "Sister")**
Mr. Chip Grant
Mrs. Leland B. Greeley (Sabella)
Mrs. Paul W. Greeley (Leila)

Mrs. William E. Green (Jackie)
Mrs. Samuel P. Greer (Sara Lynn)
Mrs. William H. Grier III (Lynn)
Mrs. James E. Hamilton, Jr. (Kandy)
Mrs. Mark A. Hamrick (Tena)
Mrs. T. Mark Hardy (Dana)
Mrs. Dana L. Harkness (Lib)
Mrs. Martin L. Hendrix (Ann)
Mrs. Doug P. Herlong (Ann)
Mrs. C. Marion Hicklin (Cathy Rose)**
Mrs. Harry E. Hicklin III (Leila)
Ms. Jocie E. Hill
Mrs. Robert R. Hill, Jr. (Carol)
Mrs. H. B. Hilton (Rosa)**
Mrs. John S. Holladay (Lora)
Mrs. James C. Holler, Jr. (Lura)
Mrs. John M. Holler (Kristi)
Mrs. Robert J. Holmes, Jr. (Nancy)
Mrs. Robert H. Hopkins (Cathie)**
Mrs. John C. Hornsby (Melanie)
Mrs. A. Watts Huckabee (Gina)
Mrs. Hiram Hutchinson (Linda)**
Mrs. John A. Johnson (Carolyn)**
Mrs. James W. Johnston (Karen)**
Ms. Virginia J. Kellett**
Mrs. Steven J. Knight (Lisa)
Mrs. Benjamin P. Knott (Norma)
Mrs. William F. Lamb (Julie)
Mrs. Mark L. Landrum (Ashley)
Mrs. C. Tony Lane (Mary Marshall
    Goode)
Mrs. Robert C. Langston (Cynthia)**
Mrs. Scott Ledford (Angie)
Mrs. David C. Leslie, Jr. (Lori)
Mrs. Richard Lewis (Mary Evelyn)
Mrs. P. David Lloyd, Jr. (Karen)
Mrs. John Lowery (Pat)
Mrs. R. H. MacKintosh (Mary Lib)**
Mrs. Essmaeil Maghsoud (Amanda)
Mrs. James M. Mahon (Daphne)
Mrs. A. F. Marshall (Harriet)**
Mrs. Thomas E. Martin (Edythe)
Mrs. Curtis Matthews (Lisa)
Mrs. Jimmie C. Matthews (Marti)

Mrs. Lerue Mayfield (Addie)
Mrs. William G. McCarthy, Jr. (Sheila)
Mrs. Stanley L. McDaniel, Jr. (Claudia)
Mrs. Michael T. McFall (Nancy)
Mrs. D. Gregory McGinnis (Becky)
Mrs. Richard A. McKenrick (Theresa)
Mrs. Thomas A. McKinney (Camille)**
Mrs. Kyle E. Melton (Robin)**
Mrs. F. Thomas Merritt, Jr. (Suzanne)
Mrs. Lawrence R. Mickle (Louise)
Mrs. J. Roddey Miller (Norma)
Mrs. Carlisle C. Moore, Jr. (Sara)
Mrs. Carlisle C. Moore III (Kathy)**
Mrs. Houston O. Motz, Jr. (Mary Ann)
Mrs. Roland F. Myers, Jr. (Jane)
Mrs. Jennings F. Neely (Harriet)
Mrs. Jennings F. Neely, Jr. (Linda)
Mrs. J. T. Neely (Louise)
Mrs. W. J. Neely, Jr. (Frances)
Mrs. Walter S. Newton (Sharon)
Mrs. Alan M. Nichols (Julia)
Mrs. Richard B. Norwood (Laura)
Mrs. Charles L. Okey Jr. (Tina)**
Mrs. Phillip C. Okey (Suzanne)**
Mrs. Scott C. Oliver (Rebecca)
Mrs. Mitchell Payne (Dee Dee)
Mrs. Burnham H. Perry (Mary)
Mrs. M. James Perry (Angie)**
Mrs. Bruce A. Peterson (Sharon)
Mrs. Jeffrey T. Pilcher (Julia)
Mrs. J. D. Pilcher, Jr. (Natalie)**
Mrs. Thomas G. Pilcher (Linda)**
Mrs. Richard O. Poag (Pam)
Mrs. John C. Pollok (Maura)
Mrs. E. Neal Powell, Jr. (Betty)
Ms. Georgeanne Pratt
Mrs. Joseph C. Raad (Lindy)
Mrs. William W. Rader (Betty)
Mrs. Pride Ratterree, Jr. (Gwen)**
Mrs. John E. Reese III (Carrie)
Mrs. J. Douglas Reynolds, Jr. (Ann)
Mrs. James C. Rhea III (Grazier)
Mrs. J. C. Rhea, Jr. (Betty Jo)**
Mrs. Samuel W. Rhodes (Sarah)

Mrs. Samuel W. Rhodes, Jr. (Julie)
Mrs. Richard L. Richter (Donna)
Mrs. John D. Rinehart, Jr. (Dee Dee)
Mrs. W. Kenneth Roddey (Sharon)
Mrs. David M. Rodgers (Dotsy)
Mrs. Carmen J. Savoca (Ann)
Mrs. Gerald E. Schapiro (Barbara)
Mrs. Christopher W. Schroeder (Lisa)
Mrs. Robert Scoville (Charlie)
Mrs. Tim Sease (Tina)
Mrs. James W. Sheedy (Elizabeth)
Mrs. E. T. Shillinglaw (Jan)
Mrs. Ragan Simpson (Judy)
Mrs. Kenneth B. Smith (Rachel)
Mrs. Robert T. Smith (Jodie Roberts)
Mrs. G. Todd Snipes (Ann)
Mrs. W. C. Spencer (Ann)**
Mrs. J. O. Spradley, Jr. (Meredith)
Mrs. E. Ned Stafford, Jr. (Gail)**
Mrs. Charles M. Sutlive (Betty)
Mrs. John D. Taylor (Diane)
Mrs. Timothy D. Templeton (Nancy)
Mrs. Craig G. Thomas (Sandra)**
Mrs. Mark D. Thomas (Teresa)
Mrs. T. Thomas (Mary Frances)**
Mrs. Drenner M. Tinsley (Marsha)
Mrs. E. Scott Turner (Gary)
Mrs. Donald Vaughn (Carolyn)
Mrs. Robert Ward (Carolyn)
Mrs. Roy E. Watkins III (Kathy)**
Mrs. Paul C. Watson, Jr. (Mary)**
Ms. Trudy M. Welborn
Mrs. James D. Welsh (Sheree)
Mrs. Forrest C. Wilkerson (Totty)
Mrs. Charles C. Williams (Linda)**
Mrs. C. Richard Williams (Sheppie)
Ms. Martha J. Williams**
Mrs. Ted Williams (Leigh)
Mrs. D. Douglas Woods (Angela)
Mrs. C. Y. Workman, Jr. (Frances)**
Mrs. Howard H. Wright, Jr. (Melissa)
Mrs. Philip E. Wright (Yolanda)
Mrs. N. F. Yorke (Lane Knox)**

**Denotes Past Presidents

RECIPE TESTERS

O ur thanks to the recipe testers and their families for their time, as well as their financial support, to guarantee the highest recipe quality possible.

Mrs. Michael R. Baker (Erin)

Mrs. John M. Barnes, Jr. (Martha)

Mrs. C. Hugh Bates (Daphne)

Mrs. Edward A. Brock (Kim)

Mrs. James C. Burnette (Melanie)

Mrs. Barry Chitwood (Cindy)

Mrs. Dennis M. Clemens (Mary)

Mrs. Michael W. Climer (Kim)

Mrs. Timothy F. Cooper (Libby)

Mrs. Cameron S. Davidson (Amy)

Mrs. Jefferson R. Dill (Laura)

Mrs. David M. Gault (Beth)

Mrs. Leland B. Greeley (Sabella)

Mrs. Samuel P. Greer (Sara Lynn)

Mrs. James E. Hamilton, Jr. (Kandy)

Mrs. Mark A. Hamrick (Tena)

Mrs. T. Mark Hardy (Dana)

Ms. Jocie E. Hill

Mrs. John M. Holler (Kristi)

Mrs. Robert J. Holmes, Jr. (Nancy)

Mrs. Joseph B. Kirkpatrick (Angela)

Mrs. William G. McCarthy, Jr. (Sheila)

Mrs. D. Gregory McGinnis (Becky)

Mrs. F. Thomas Merritt, Jr. (Suzanne)

Mrs. Carlisle C. Moore III (Kathy)

Mrs. Richard B. Norwood (Laura)

Mrs. Scott C. Oliver (Rebecca)

Mrs. M. James Perry (Angie)

Mrs. Bruce A. Peterson (Sharon)

Mrs. Jeffrey T. Pilcher (Julia)

Mrs. Richard O. Poag (Pam)

Mrs. John C. Pollok (Maura)

Mrs. Robert T. Prochaska (Carrie)

Mrs. John E. Reese III (Carrie)

Mrs. Samuel W. Rhodes, Jr. (Julie)

Mrs. James W. Sheedy (Elizabeth)

Mrs. Christopher A. Taylerson (Beth)

Mrs. E. Scott Turner (Gary)

INDEX

The Junior Welfare League of Rock Hill

P.O. Box 3211
Rock Hill, South Carolina 29732
www.juniorwelfareleague.com

Please send _____ copies of *Tapestry* at $19.95 each . . . $ _____

Postage and handling at $3.00 each . . . . $ _____

Total . . . . $ _____

_____
Name

_____
Address

_____
City   State   Zip

_____
Telephone Number

Please make check payable to
The Junior Welfare League of Rock Hill.

Proceeds from the sale of *Tapestry* benefit the
York County agencies supported by the Junior Welfare League
of Rock Hill, South Carolina.

Photocopies will be accepted.